Adults in College
A Survival Guide for
Nontraditional Students

Revised Edition

Wanda Schindley, PhD

DallasPublishing Mt. Pleasant

ADULTS IN COLLEGE: A SURVIVAL GUIDE FOR
NONTRADITIONAL STUDENTS. Copyright © 1992, 2002 by Wanda
Schindley. All rights reserved. For information, address Dallas Publishing
Company, P. O. Box 1144, Mt. Pleasant, Texas 75456-1144.
editor@DallasPublishing.com
orders@DallasPublishing.com
www.DallasPublishing.com

Cover design: Kim Wommack
Illustrations: Mike Krone
"An Open Letter to the Class of 1996 UNCW," © 1996,
by Charlie Daniels. Reprinted with permission.

Printed in the United States of America

Library of Congress Control Number: 2001095841

Publisher's Cataloging-in-Publication
(Provided by Quality Books, Inc.)

Schindley, Wanda.
   Adults in college : a survival guide for
  Nontraditional students / Wanda Schindley. – Rev. ed.
   p. cm.
   Includes bibliographical references and index.
   LCCN 2001095841
   ISBN 0-912011-59-9 (hardcover)
   ISBN 0-912011-61-0 (softcover)

   1. College student orientation—United States.
2. Adult college students—United States.   1. Title.

LB2343.32.S35 2002   378.1'98'0973
                           QBI01-201236

Contents

Acknowledgements

Thanks to Diane Hudson, Charlie Daniels, Edith Wynne, Judy Taylor, Charlene Rodgers, Brad Price, and Debbie Rogers for their contributions and permission; to Lisa LeMole, Holly A. Harrill, and Ludy Gibson for their editorial help; to Kathy Zwerneman, Patsy Armstrong, Myra McGinnis, Cathy Worth, Edith McKinney and the many other adult students who contributed stories, time, and input; to Diane Motz, Mike Krone, and Kim Wommack for cover designs and artwork; to my husband Ken Schindley for his patience and support, and to the late Dr. Diane Dodson Hudson who inspired students and colleagues alike.

Chapter 1

Why You Belong in College

Do you remember the words "love is wasted on the young" from the old song "The Second Time Around"? I have often thought the same thing about college. The thought occurs to me when I face a roomful of 18-year-old freshmen and respond to questions such as "Will we have any homework?" and "Do we have to answer *all* the questions?" and "Do we have to come to class, or can we just show up for the exams?" The transition from high school to college for traditional students is a process that involves maturing and prioritizing, a process that sometimes lasts several years. Understandably, college freshmen try the same excuses that worked in high school—"I have to work part-time (sob)"; "I lost $20 on a football game, and I was too depressed (sob) to do the paper"; "I have allergies (cough, cough)"; "My computer crashed" (an updated version of " My dog ate my paper, but it *can* happen").

For many traditional students, college is merely four more years of high school with increased freedom to party. And many students who did well in high school by memorizing facts the night before an exam are shattered when the technique fails to work in college. So they need an extra day or two for the next major paper or test. They get this extra time when their grandmothers die. (Grandmothers of college freshmen die at an alarming rate. In fact, some grandmothers die several times. Remarkable.)

On the other hand, I have rarely heard whines or excuses from adult students. (I will use the term *adult student* to refer to college students over the age of 25). I have had adult students who were raising families, working full-time, taking three or four courses, dealing with the IRS, divorce lawyers, dentist bills, etc., and (I assume) keeping some kind of order in their homes. Do these students hand in late papers or miss exams? I don't think the possibility even occurs to them. If an adult student misses a class, I worry. If a paper is due and isn't delivered by a friend or the Federal Express man, I assume the student is in the hospital in a coma or a full body cast. I have had adult students fax their papers to me or send friends or family members to deliver papers to me. I have been notified as much as three months in advance that an adult student will be absent on a certain day because of a job-, spouse-, or child-related event. Adult students want to know in advance what they need to do to make up for absences. They worry about missing class. They truly regret missing class.

Furthermore, when adult students miss class, they are missed. Most college instructors are delighted to see older faces in their classes. Older students add a depth to class discussion that can only come from experience—from having lived and coped, tried and failed, tried and succeeded, and survived. And the instructors are not the only ones who are enriched by the presence of adult, or non-traditional, students. Although it is a common fear among older students that the young students in the class will snub them or even ridicule them, I have found the reverse to be true. Young students often try to sit by older students and look to them for various kinds of support. They depend on older students to answer questions the instructor throws out, to hear and write down assignments, to be leaders in group work, and to offer insight and first-hand knowledge about events that happened before they were born.

Patsy Armstrong, a 42-year-old who started back to college as her son was entering the same school, said she had never imagined that she would develop friendships with young people the age of her children. She said, "The young people help those of us who are older stay young, and I like to think that we have a good influence on them." Patsy quoted one young woman as saying that before her relationships with adults in college, she had "never been spoken to by an adult without feeling that the adult was talking down to [her]."

Patsy also noted that she has a changed relationship with her own children. She now has conversations with her kids about math, science, college professors, and learning in general instead of the old close-the-refrigerator diatribe. She also said the family has learned to cope with a dirtier kitchen. Now, both she and the kids respond to the call of dirty dishes with "But I have homework to do."

At first her presence at the same college was difficult for her son. "I had invaded his territory," she said. "He didn't really want to be around me at school, but by the end of the first year we were taking classes together and had the same group of classmate friends. We began to see each other as people, not just mom and son. We became friends."

I think Patsy's experiences with young people are typical, given enough time and exposure. Patsy attends a small community college, however, where friendly interaction is the rule rather than the exception. In larger schools, there is perhaps more segregation of age groups. Young students may be reluctant to speak out in class and to interact with older students when they feel their peers might not approve. Traditional freshmen may still be overly concerned about what their peers think of them. In fact, you may find yourself in classes where the young students refuse to open their mouths because of fear of ridicule, and the older students end up doing all the talking. It's not that young people don't have anything to say; they are afraid of what their peers will think and, sometimes, intimidated by the professors. (Becoming old enough to not be ruled by peer pressure is wonderfully liberating.)

Yes, there is a possibility that you will get an icy stare from a traditional freshman has not been properly socialized or who hates your guts for raising the grade curve on an exam. But don't take it personally. Today's 40- to 50-year-olds can remember they were young at a time when the prevailing teenage wisdom was, "Don't trust anyone over 30." (The result, I think, was hellacious 30th birthdays for many. Turning 40? Eh, it was nothing compared to turning 30.)

I'm not suggesting that *all* traditional students are immature and should work at McDonald's for a couple of years before they enter college. Some students are ready for college immediately after high school. These students are motivated internally to succeed, and they have a tight rein on their hormones. Although their hip classmates may call them "nerds", they are serious about learning and are the leaders of the future. But for many students, college is ancillary to other things that are happening in their lives. They are searching for a mate, a niche, and a way to get the "stuff" that our society has taught them is all-important. They are often impatient and eager to try their wings in the Real World, and there is nothing wrong with that. Many students attend college for a semester or two, drop out to marry or start earning a paycheck, and return to college later when they have set specific goals.

Note: My experience has been with traditional students at a state university and a community college. The more prestigious universities attract more students who are serious about college at a young age. These students have proven themselves in high school and have a higher rate of graduation than do students entering state universities and community colleges.

Who are the Nontraditional Students?

Adults are attending college in record numbers. Some begin college for the first time as adults, while others return to finish what they started as teenagers. Of more than 14 million students in the nation's colleges, about 40% are over age 24.

College Enrollment (in millions)[1]

	1983	1993	1995[2]	2002[3]
Total	12,462	14,762	13,913	15,206
Under 25 years of age	7,400	8,219	7,818	8,899
25 years and over	5,062	6,543	6,095	6,307
Men				
14-24 years old	3,757	3,969	3,690	4,136
25 years and over	2,268	2,675	2,495	2,469
Total	6,025	6,644	6,185	6,605
Women				
14-24 years old	3,643	4,250	4,120	4,762
25 years and over	2,794	3,868	3,600	3,838
Total	6,437	8,118	7,720	8,600

[1]Statistics from NCES   [2]Estimated   [3]Projected

In 1993 and again in the year 2002, according to projections by the National Center for Educational Statistics, almost 4 million women over the age of 25 will be enrolled in college. The dramatic increase between 1983 and 1993 in enrollment of women over age 25 represented the largest increase among sex and age groups. Although more adult students than younger students enroll part-time, their presence in sheer numbers is having a real impact. Colleges have begun depending on them and addressing their needs.

Twenty years ago, the term *non-traditional* was used mainly to describe the 18- to 21-year-olds who were taking vocational education courses in such fields as heating and air conditioning, printing, electronics, etc. Yet the term was also used to describe older students who were taking courses, often given off-campus in industrial settings, as part of retraining or "continuing education" programs. The adult students were usually not seeking degrees or changes in careers but were simply doing what they had to do to maintain their positions.

Today, the term *non-traditional* is used most often to describe the full- or part-time student who is more than 25 years of age. Why is age 25 the dividing line? I don't know. Perhaps it has to do with the same statistics that result in higher automobile insurance for young people under the age of 25 and that tell us most violent crimes are committed by people under 25 years of age. Statistical differences of all sorts indicate an increase in stability after the age of 25. Perhaps, then, reality is not so clouded by passions. At any rate, most schools do not require SAT or ACT scores of enrolling students who are more than 25 years of age because those students are more likely to be successful students, regardless of their high school grades or standardized test scores. These adult students may start out "under-prepared" in some areas, but they tend to catch up quickly.

While doing research for this book, I talked to scores of men and women who were currently enrolled in college. Many of them had reached dead ends in their careers and were entering or re-entering college to gain skills and knowledge (and degrees) that would make them more valuable (and promotable) to their companies or to qualify for new, higher-paying, more prestigious careers. Many had not graduated from high school but were, as adults, determined and successful students. Some already had satisfying careers but wanted the personal satisfaction of earning a college degree. Others were taking classes for the pure joy of learning and didn't really care about a degree.

I talked to single parents who were using their meager resources to attend college because they wanted to make better lives for themselves and for their children. I talked to men and women who, because of death, divorce, job loss, etc., had experienced drastic changes in their lives. I talked to men and women who were retired or who had already raised their families and now had time to do what they had wanted to do for so long. I asked them questions such as "Why are you now in college?" and "Why didn't you go (or finish) right after high school?" Many of them had stories similar to my own, so I will share with you my journey.

I was 28 when I first started college. Why didn't I go to college right after high school? Rampant hormones, I suppose. I wanted to experience all those things I had read about. I was in love, and I wanted freedom. I had been bored in high school and fairly chomping at the bit to become independent and get away from rules and rule-mongers. I have often wondered whether I would have even graduated if I hadn't, after being expelled from study hall as a freshman and having to take a sixth course, discovered that I could graduate a year early if I took six courses each semester and attended summer school. I made a plan and stuck with it. I graduated; packed my clothes, portable typewriter, Gregg typing book, hi-fi, and records; stuffed my bra with the $50 I had saved working part-time at a health club; and hopped a Greyhound to North Carolina where my fiancé was stationed for Vietnam indoctrination. The only marketable skill I took with me was 40-words-per-minute typing.

After I had found a $12 per week efficiency apartment (yes, I'm dating myself), I started pounding the pavement. In between applying for and being turned down for jobs, I practiced my typing. Then I answered an ad for secretary at the local newspaper. I really wanted to be a journalist apprentice, but in my desperation, *secretary* sounded pretty good. (So did *waitress*, but I wasn't experienced—so I was told.)

I had taken shorthand in high school, but was certainly no natural at it. At any rate, I took a dictation test, broke out in hives—even before I tried unsuccessfully to read the scribbles back, and was quickly channeled into the composing room for a typing test. I landed a job as a teletypesetter-operator apprentice. When I left North Carolina, I took a journeyman test and became a printer. The job allowed me to travel and to make more money than teachers, nurses, and most of the journalists at the newspapers. But I still wanted to be a writer, and somewhere along the line, I acquired a burning desire to go to college. I also acquired the maturity it takes to appreciate the idea of and the fact of college.

So, after an eleven-year career as a typesetter and nine years of marriage, I enrolled at a junior college. Scared spitless and knowing I was risking my marriage and my self-concept, I dug in. I took all the television and self-paced courses I could fit into my self-made degree plan, attended classes, and discovered that humans can survive on very little sleep. That was the beginning of my infatuation with college. I completed a two-year degree program in a little more than one year and spent the next eight years earning a bachelor's degree, two master's degrees, and, finally, a doctorate. After teaching at high school, college, and adult education levels; writing and directing grant programs; and writing textbook material for all levels, including a college textbook, I decided to enroll in some sociology courses for fun. My husband was going out-of-state to polygraph examiner school for ten weeks, and I wanted to make sure my evenings were full. My compulsive-student nature kicked in, and I earned another master's degree that I didn't take because I decided to apply the courses to a second doctorate. I have now finished all course work for a doctorate in sociology, and the journey has been wonderful.

When I started college at age 28, I was ready for college; ten years earlier, I was not. Had I had the opportunity to go, someone pushing me and paying for college, I might have succeeded, but I am sure I would not have had the same experience at age 18. I would not have gotten the most from college because I would not have put forth the effort that I was prepared to put forth at age 28. Now, I'm almost 50, and I have been a student for most of my life, and I plan to be for the rest of my life in one way or another.

But I've left out an important part of my educational experience. Before I enrolled in college, I mentioned to a friend at work that I worried about this and that aspect of college—whether or not "they" would let me do this or that, whether I had to have a degree plan, and so forth. My friend Kyle, who had just finished an associate degree program, said, "Your attitude is all wrong. You're letting the idea of college intimidate you. You are an adult. You are self-supporting. You make decisions daily. You know who you are. You're a citizen, a taxpayer—you help support that school and pay the salaries of those who work there. You also pay tuition. Think of it as buying a service. You are a *customer*. 'They' are there for *you*. However, the rules, the programs, are all designed for eighteen-year-olds who need guidance to get from here to there. But you, as an adult, can go in and tell them what you want and get it. They put their pants on one leg at a time, too."

I remember Kyle's advice well; I was old enough to see the logic in it and to make good use of it. Many times I have recalled his words when I felt insignificant (or dumped on), and the words helped me to recoup my self-esteem and sense of purpose—to go for it. I rank his advice right up there with that of Polonius to his son Laertes when the latter started to college (in Shakespeare's *Hamlet*):

. . . The wind sits in the shoulder of your sail,
And you are stayed for. There—my blessings with thee,
And these few precepts in thy memory look thou
    character.

Translation: Good luck, but let me give you some advice
               before you leave.

Give thy thoughts no tongue,
Nor any unproportioned [unbalanced] thought his act.

Translation: Think before you speak, and think long and
               hard before you act.

Be thou familiar, but by no means vulgar.
Those friends thou hast, and their adoption tried,
Grapple them unto thy soul with hoops of steel,
But do not dull thy palm with entertainment
Of each new-hatched, unfledged courage
    [gallant youth].

Translation: Be friendly, but keep your distance, and don't
               fall in with the wrong crowd and do stupid
               stuff.

Beware of entrance to a quarrel; but being in,
Bear't that th' opposed may beware of thee.

Translation: Don't be quick to fight, but stand your ground
               when you must.

Give every man thine ear, but few thy voice;
Take each man's censure [opinion], but reserve thy
    judgment.

Translation: Listen more than you talk.
    Costly thy habit [clothes] as thy purse can buy,
    But not expressed in fancy; rich, not gaudy,
    For the apparel oft proclaims the man,
    And they in France of the best rank and station
    Are of a most select and generous, chief in that
    [show their taste and good breeding chiefly in dress].

Translation: Don't dress like a teeny-bopper. (But be
                grateful for the universality of and comfort of
                jeans.)

Neither a borrower nor a lender be,
For loan oft loses both itself and friend,
And borrowing dulleth edge of husbandry [thrift].
This above all, to thine own self be true,
And it must follow, as the night the day,

Thou canst not then be false to any man. . . .
                            (Shakespeare, *Hamlet* I.iii.)

(I will not defile the final section with a translation.
Shakespeare's words are too fine.)

Mature students are patient enough to listen to advice,
know how much they don't know, and enjoy the learning
journey. They can truly appreciate the college experience.
Adult students have the advantage of maturity.

Although adult students are at various stages in their lives
and have different goals, they have one thing in common: they

are all making sacrifices to attend college. The single mother who, after working all day, listens to her toddler cry as she leaves for class, the father who feels guilty about spending his off-work time studying instead of with his children, and the retiree who no longer has time for friends and family or to bake or babysit or yard work are all sacrificing their time. They are also sacrificing their money. Most adult students are paying for their educations; they are self-supporting. Mom and Dad are not footing the bill, and many adult students are sacrificing something other than time and money: They are sacrificing harmony in their homes.

Counselors talk about "contracts," the unspoken "deals" that are struck as couples adjust to married life. If going to college was not an expected part of a couple's life together, the spouse who decides to enter college must try to renegotiate the contract. Some partners do not want to renegotiate; they prefer to keep the status quo and proceed to make life miserable for the college-bound spouse. Even if the spouse is supportive, he or she isn't always happy about it all. By this I mean that a spouse may be supportive on a rational level and even say all the right things ("Yes, I think it's wonderful that you are going to school") and still have emotional relapses (an expression of pitiful neglect when dinner is not on the table or when a student spouse is too tired to go out on a special occasion). Such reactions from spouses or even (or especially) kids cause adult students to feel guilty and result in minor, or even major, disruption in the home. (See Chapter 2 for more on this topic.)

Adult students also share other characteristics: They are settled; they are responsible; they are serious about learning. And they are human—older and wiser—but human, anyway: very often they are STRESSED-OUT.

Because adult students are making sacrifices, because they are paying for their own education, because they feel their identities are somehow related to how well they do in school, because they are treading in unfamiliar waters, because they are so responsible, they have a tendency toward obsessive-compulsive behavior and, consequently, mega-stress—even to the detriment of their health. They are perfectionists and feel personally inadequate when they make mistakes. Whereas traditional students are quicker to "blow off" a poor performance (there *will* be another day) and, perhaps, blame a failure on someone or something else, the adult student will worry and fret and perceive every minute of class and study time as the "zero hour."

Of course, most adult students have full and stressful lives without the added stresses of college, but college to many adults is much more stressful than it need be. To illustrate, one of my students is a pastor's wife (her duties require as much time as a full-time job) and mother of three young children. She spent an evening away from her family to use the church typewriter to type a paper (which was twice as long as was expected) for my class. She returned home, found a couple of errors in the paper, went back to the church, and worked until after midnight retyping a perfect copy. She was not a fast typist.

Now, she is certainly an exemplary student; however, the stress she endured to produce a perfect paper was unnecessary for these reasons: (1.) I did not require that the paper be typed (although it is usually a good idea). (2.) I encouraged students to proofread and make neat, hand-written corrections on their final drafts in class before handing them in.

I was not thrilled that the woman spent so much time on the paper; I felt guilty (for what, I'm not sure) and dismayed. I say and do many things in my classes for the purpose of reducing my students' stress, and I was sorry to see energy spent unnecessarily. I don't, however, want to give the impression that correctness, attention to detail, and going beyond the basic requirements of an assignment is bad. I will say more about this in Chapter 5. Throughout this book, I will give suggestions for saving time and reducing stress and will, I hope, help you to differentiate between necessary and unnecessary stress, between the important and the unimportant.

Why you belong in college

The simple answer is that you are ready to enjoy the experience and grow from it. Whether you are interested in enrolling in a non-credit craft class or taking a full load of academic classes, you will benefit from the process of learning. You are ready for college. Perhaps you were not when you were younger. Perhaps family obligations or an unsupportive spouse made attending college impossible. Perhaps it just wasn't a priority then. But now, you are ready. You have a desire, an interest, or you would not be reading this book. You want to be a learner, and you want to achieve a goal. The goal may be to take one course in a subject that interests you or to earn a degree to qualify for a particular job. You are ready to work toward your goal. You have lived and matured and experienced different kinds of joys and pains. You have been in school, all right—life's school. Now you are ready for college, ready to prove to your family and friends that you can do it—you can succeed in college. But most importantly you are ready to prove to yourself you can do it.

Will you be the oldest person in class?

You may have noticed that the youth culture of the past is waning. You see models with wrinkles in television commercials, and you see more commercials for products purchased by older adults. In fact, the foremost business of the future will be taking care of the health and beauty needs of 69 million baby boomers who will not "go quietly into that good night." They will fight the aging process with everything they have. Don Henley summed up the philosophy of the baby boom generation nicely when he said, "You don't quit playing music when you get old. You get old when you quit playing music." Baby boomers refuse to get "old." They seem to be in the process of redefining the concept, and they are being helped along by the fact that today's youth do not resent them on the scale they resented their parents' generation. The baby boomers' music, for example, is widely appreciated by today's youth, but you wouldn't have caught baby boomers in their youth listening to Benny Goodman or Bing Crosby.

Because of the sheer number of baby boomers and, of course, the power they hold in media, their cultural innovations are being recycled. On the other hand, the birth rate in America has been declining for a number of years. In 1980 there were more than 16 million 18 to 21 year olds; in 1990 there were fewer than 12 million. The over-thirty age group now constitutes the majority of the population, has most of the money, and is on the move, in record numbers, to college.

So, chances are, you will not be the oldest one in your classes. And if you are, you will probably be the only one to notice. The kids are preoccupied with their own fears and dreams. But you, when you really get a grip on your fears, will realize that nothing will happen to you in college that is more traumatic than what you've already lived through. Will an exam, for instance, be worse than labor pains or a hemorrhoidectomy or a ruptured disk? No. You're old enough to know that an exam is merely a challenge, and you're old enough to enjoy it—on some level at least. That's not to say you've blown it entirely if you feel uptight about an exam. Normal "uptight" and "out-of-control-uptight" are two different things.

Before my best friend died, she made a statement that I recall often. She said, "I wish I hadn't lived my life by fear and definition." She was very successful—a wonderful teacher, writer, human being, but she still felt controlled by the fear of not living up to the expectations of others. I'm sharing this with hope that you will relate her words to your own life, as I have to mine.

Ludy Gibson, who finished college at a break-neck speed while managing a household (husband and two children) and caring for her mother, warns others to slow down and enjoy the journey. Her advice is "Don't think because you are an older student that you have to rush through it to make up for lost time. It is not a race to see who finishes first." She also advises not to be discouraged from starting college with the thought that college is a four-year commitment, by which time you will be four years older. If you don't start now, you will still be four years older in four years. If you do start now, you could have a major life accomplishment under your belt in four years.

Will you be the dumbest person in class?

Eric Hoffer, the "longshoreman philosopher" who had little formal education, said, "In a time of drastic change it is the learners who inherit the future. The learned usually find themselves equipped to live in a world that no longer exists."

We are living in a time of drastic change, and flexibility is required to adapt. The changes over the last ten years in technology have left many adults asking their children to program new VCRs or telephones. Still, today's adults have witnessed more change in a shorter period of time than any previous generation, and they have survived. You have survived. You may not be "learned" by an academic definition, but you probably are a learner.

Formal education does not make one a learner. When Charlie Daniels was asked to speak to the graduating class at the University of North Carolina at Wilmington, a couple of students called Daniels a "one-hit wonder" and "goober-brained red-neck" in the college newspaper. Daniels responded with a wonderful letter. I included the letter in my college English textbook, *The Informed Citizen: Argument and Analysis*, and I will include it here.

An Open Letter to the Class of 1996 UNCW
By Charlie Daniels

I would like to clear up a few points about my addressing your class at the commencement exercises, points which I feel have been distorted by a few overzealous, uninformed pseudo journalists.

I will not address the "one hit wonder," "goober brained redneck" aspect of these pieces, and one letter published in *The Seahawk* I will not address at all except to say that the racial overtones it contained were totally unfounded and offensive beyond description.

My professional life is a matter of documented public record and easily obtainable. No need to discuss that.

First of all, this is not the first time I have been invited to speak to a graduating class at UNCW. I have been approached for the past couple of years, but due to prearranged commitments I have been unable to accept.

Having been born in Wilmington, I consider it an honor to be asked to speak to you on one of the biggest days of your lives, and I accepted the honor with gratitude and humility. I cannot speak to you of lofty academic ideals nor scholarly pursuits because I have neither entree nor credential for that world.

The truth is I come to you from the street, from reality, the very same place you're all headed if you plan to make a living in this ever-changing, difficult, show-me world, and when your college days are just a memory and your diploma hangs beneath dusty glass or on some office wall, you will still have to deal with that world on its own terms every working day of your lives.

Let me tell you why I thought I was invited to speak to your graduating class. My career spans almost 40 years and you don't go through 40 years of hard work and unrelenting competition without learning a few things.

My qualifications are humble, but extensive and diverse. I've stood at the 38th Parallel and looked across into the hostile eyes of the North Korean border guards. I've been catapulted from the deck of an aircraft carrier in the middle of the Adriatic Sea and ridden across the frozen wastes of Greenland on an Eskimo dog sled. I've taken a hammer and chisel to the Berlin Wall and performed with symphony orchestras. I've had conversations with presidents and walked the halls of Congress lobbying for legislation in which I believe. I've flown on the Concorde and acted in motion pictures. I've seen the royal palaces of Europe and the hovels of Hong Kong.

I've seen the Mona Lisa and stared in awe at the timeless works of Vincent Van Gogh. I've gathered cattle in the Big Bend country of Texas and met some of the wisest people I know at campfires in the middle of nowhere. I've been privileged to have conversations with Alex Haley and Louis L'Amour. I've appeared with the Rolling Stones, worked in the recording studio with Bob Dylan and two of the Beatles. I've been married to the same woman for over 30 years and raised a son who did, by the way, go to college. I've kept 20 people gainfully and steadily employed for over 20 years.

I am not a man of letters; I readily admit that. But is being a man of letters the only thing which qualifies one to speak to a group of men and women who are about to enter the real world? My world.

My address will not be delivered in the beautiful strains of poetry of a Maya Angelou or with the technical expertise of a Tom Clancy, but I can tell you where some of the land mines are hidden, the shortest path to the top of the mountain and the quickest way down. Been there, done that.

Thank you and God bless the Class of '96.

Daniels' letter illustrates so well the value of experience. Although you may be in awe of Daniels' exciting life, you have had other experiences from which you have learned and grown. You are experienced, and you've been to the college of living. You may take for granted much of what you know and may feel that your knowledge borders on the insignificant— after all, you don't know calculus or trigonometry or quantum mechanics. And the kids right out of high school know about gerunds and cognates. And what will you do if the instructor asks you a question about something you've forgotten?

It may be encouraging to you to know that many of the things you learned in school and forgot over the years were not important in the first place. For instance, you probably spent a great deal of time learning to diagram sentences and practicing that skill—even agonizing over where a particular phrase fit into the grand scheme. Researchers now (in fact, some research dates from 1910) tell us that "discrete item" grammar instruction (diagramming or parsing sentences), learning grammar for the sake of learning grammar, is not helpful in making students better writers and may, in fact, produce worse writers because of the time taken away from actual writing practice. So, if you're worried about forgetting the meaning of a term such as "retained object," don't. It is unlikely that you could find even a professional writer who knows or cares what the term means. Good writing takes practice. (Read all about it in Chapter 7.)

And in history class you may find that remembering the date of the completion of the transcontinental railroad is not as important as understanding the social and economical significance. From your life experience (which includes juggling finances) you have a fuller context in which to plug the facts than an 18 year old, and new information is better retained when it is associated with, or plugged into, existing information and perceptions. While younger students may be accustomed to memorizing facts for objective exams (and quickly forgetting them afterward), you will probably prefer essay exams in which you will have a chance to demonstrate your understanding of concepts and the significance of and relationships among events.

Survival Tip: Reading List

To jumpstart your brain in preparation for college learning, read, read, read. Below are suggestions to kick in higher order thinking processes. For nonfiction try

- *A Pen Warmed up in Hell: Mark Twain in Protest*, a collection of short social writings. (There was never a more impassioned social critic than Twain. That his late works are not read and that his fiction is being banned from school libraries are horrifying.)
- Robert B. Downs' *Books That Changed the World* tells about and gives excerpts from 27 of the most important works ever written. Even if you don't manage to wade through the entire book, you will be miles ahead if you read at least a few pages about each work.
- Aristotle's *Rhetoric* (Start with the fascinating section on why people commit crimes, Chapter 2, section 1368, second sentence.)
- P. J. O'Rourke's *Holidays in Hell* is a brilliantly written journey through foreign countries that is also hilarious at times. O'Rourke sometimes has articles in *Rolling Stone*

magazine. His articles on Somolia, the former Yugoslavia, and Haiti are worth looking up. William Greider is another excellent *Rolling Stone* writer. It's worth subscribing to the magazine and suffering the embarrassment of having the mail person deliver magazines with half-naked people on the cover to read O'Rourke's and Greider's occasional pieces. (The same goes for *Vanity Fair*'s Christopher Hitchens and Dominick Dunne.)

- Thorstein Veblen's *The Theory of the Leisure Class.* You may want to do some judicious skimming, but his theory is classic and relevant.
- Eric Hoffer's *The True Believer*–a fast read.
- My college English textbook (*The Informed Citizen: Argument and Analysis*, Harcourt Brace) contains a wealth of short, thought-provoking readings and intensive help with writing.

For lighter reading, try novels that range from the bizarre to the prophetic such as

- Tom Robbins' *Skinny Legs and All*
- Jack London's *Call of the Wild*
- James Michner's *The Source*
- Twain's *A Connecticut Yankee in King Arthur's Court*
- Aldous Huxley's *Brave New World*
- George Orwell's *1984* (most important!)

When you watch television, try watching

- The History Channel
- A&E (especially *Biography* and *Ancient Mysteries*)
- The Discovery Channel and The Learning Channel

Other fears

You may also worry that you have forgotten how to study or that you will make a fool of yourself or that you will appear stupid in front of a class of preppies. Don't. You can brush up on the study skills (see chapters 2 and 6), and as for making a fool of yourself—well, everything's relative. You can worry and fret about everything you say and do, but you have no control over how others perceive those actions and words. Am I safe in assuming that you will not streak through the student lounge wearing nothing but Reeboks or interrupt a discussion about the history of the Civil War to tell a dirty joke or pick your nose while giving a presentation? Okay, then. Yes, those things are unacceptable, but you will not be doing them. So, anything short of those things will probably not even raise an eyebrow. So what if you mispronounce a word or wear your skirts longer than anyone else in the class or sneeze and pop the button off your pants? The truth of the matter is this: If others *do* notice, they will not give it a second thought. And saying something that is off-the-wall or just plain stupid is part of life; undoubtedly, the speaker remembers the statement far longer than the listeners.

Survival tip

Keep your sense of humor. If you don't have one, get one.

You may say or do something in class that brings laughter. If so, enjoy the fact that you have been entertaining and join in the laughter. A sense of humor can help you through the most embarrassing situation.

Remember also, the pressure you feel to act appropriately is much stronger in adolescents. To an adolescent, peer approval is necessary for a healthy self-concept. Adolescents generally find it harder to laugh at themselves than adults. You are old enough to know that what other people think is secondary to what you think of yourself, your goals, and your future.

Why you are ready for college

For traditional students, newly released from the rules and mandates of parents and high school teachers, college offers a less-structured environment than they have experienced before or will experience later in the Real World. To adolescents, however, adults seem to have all the freedom anyone needs. Adults make the rules and enforce them. But adults know the pressures of having to show up for work when they feel like staying in bed, of having to put up with a nasty boss because they need the job, and of being responsible to others. The common misconception of many adolescents is that when they reach adulthood, they won't have to answer to anyone. Bless their hearts—they think Mom and Dad are suffering from dementia when they wistfully comment on the carefreedom of young people. They think Mom and Dad are lying when they say the familiar lines, "You don't have a care in the world. Just wait until you have a family of your own."

In college, adolescents must be responsible and must grow up in a hurry. They must learn to budget their time and fulfill their obligations without being told when to do homework, when to go to bed, when to eat, when they can play. They don't have parents and teachers standing over their shoulders with offers of help and guidance. Consequently, almost half of the traditional students entering college fail to graduate, and most of that half drop out in the first year.

We don't know how well Laertes heeded his father's advice, but we can be sure that most young people want to learn from experience. Sure, they pay the price, as we stand there shaking our heads and pleading for them to listen, but they are just as entitled to have the fun of making their own mistakes as we were. Often young people are too impatient to even listen to the wisdom of age, and, frankly, they aren't really sure how to go about determining the difference between wisdom and b.s.

Contrary to many 18-year-olds, you already know that the "equal opportunity" so loudly touted is based on how much effort one is willing to put forth. You already know that you can save yourself a lot of trouble by listening to the advice of others. And you already know that it is socially unacceptable (and possibly dangerous) to express *all* your views about others. You have already learned to tolerate on some level, if not respect, the views and experience of others. And what you have learned will be of immeasurable value to you as an adult in college. You will know, for instance, that those kids who have pierced tongues or other somewhat grotesque add-ons will be simply trying to make statements. They may not be sure what statement they want to make—that will come later—but they are still from this planet and just as normal and friendly as those who are more conservative.

What college will do for you

First, think about what college will *not* do for you. College will not make you a learner if you choose to get by with the minimum effort. Many students are focused on the degree and memorize what they must and forget it after a test—a kind of garbage in, garbage out routine. There is nothing wrong with being single-minded about a degree if you need to reach a goal in a given period of time. But as you struggle through to meet the demands of this or that class, develop a curiosity about what you are doing at the time. Open yourself to the peripheral and make notes to explore later the things that seem interesting. For instance, when reading a chapter in an introductory sociology text, you read that Emile Durkheim did a study of suicide that is still used today. You think it sounds really interesting, and you want to know more about it. Make a note to check out the book or to read about the study in an advanced text when you have time over the holidays. Or better yet, write it on a list of interesting topics you can explore when you have to write a research paper. Don't limit yourself to what you learn in the classroom. College should be a license to learn, to explore beyond the classroom. College will introduce you to many topics and concepts that you can then research on your own.

Whether you are going to college to qualify for a better job or to fulfill a long-time desire, you will be enriched in many unexpected ways. Through interactions with others, your scope and perspective will grow. Through interactions with text you, perhaps, had never before even heard of, your understanding of others and the world will be broadened. You will find a subject area that interests you more than others, and you may find that you were born to be an archeologist, a psychologist, or whatever. You will find that you are capable of much more than you had imagined when you worried about whether you had what it takes to succeed in college.

If you are now in the workforce but are dissatisfied with your occupation or expect technological advances to eventually make your job obsolete, college can arm you with the skills needed for a new career. You have probably heard a lot about the changing face of the future workforce. For instance, analysts predict that in the near future, 19-21 percent of data management work will be done in the home and transferred through modem and fax. The jobs that now require a minimal level of skills are being eliminated while the jobs that are added—other than minimum-wage, fast-food jobs— require a higher skill level. Manufacturing and even mid-management jobs are being eliminated daily as companies downsize. Among jobs listed as good for the future are many different positions related to health care. *The Occupational Handbook* (available at most libraries) provides in-depth information if you want to choose a future career based on future prospects and average salaries. The table below uses data from the *Digest of Educational Statistics* and *Infoplease*. The figures change from year to year and are included here mainly for comparison. Note the difference in average salaries for degreed and non-degreed median annual incomes. Also, note the difference in salaries for men and women. Much has been made of this difference. Some people use the difference to support the argument that women are still victims of rampant discrimination. Other people attribute the difference to the fact that women are primary family caregivers and may serve for a shorter time in the workforce, perhaps entering a career position later or taking time out of a career to have children.

Education and Earnings

	H.S. grad.	Assoc. degree	Bachelor's degree	Master's degree	Professional	Doctorate
M	$27,370	$33,690	$42,757	$51,867	$80,549	$63,149
F	19,963	23,056	31,197	38,612	50,211	47,249

Again, what you get from college depends a great deal on your goals and your attitudes about learning. You can go through the motions and become enriched only to the extent necessary to get a degree. On the other hand, some people never get the piece of paper but still are seekers and forever enriched by their college experiences. In fact, some people take mostly non-credit courses with no thoughts of earning degrees and still find new life interests or commitments. Through a non-credit class in china painting, for instance, a previously undiscovered artistic talent may bloom. I know a woman who started china painting when she was 65 years old. She had never believed she was even artistically inclined, let alone extremely talented. Within a couple of years, she was teaching others the art of china painting.

A single class or an entire program can lead you in a direction for self-study even when the course work itself is sadly lacking in real content. For instance, teachers often complain that education courses in college do not prepare them for the classroom. A new teacher often learns more in the first six-week period than in the entire course of education study. In college, however, you will be introduced to resources you can explore on your own—the books and journals related to just about any field of interest.

So college opens the doors; real seekers of knowledge go far beyond the entrance—perhaps to the extent that in some field, in spite of your college work, you will still consider yourself self-educated. Whether college helps you land a new job, makes you feel better about your self, or stimulates you and provides an impetus for life-long learning, you will grow in other ways and find unexpected benefits. One woman told me that she had lost 30 pounds since she started taking college courses. She said going to college had been the best diet program she had ever tried.

Chapter 2
Overcoming Obstacles and Special Circumstances

If you dropped out of high school

Many people dropped out of high school when they were young for the same reasons others finished high school but did not go on to college. A survey of GED candidates, people who are preparing to take an exam for a high school equivalency diploma, showed the following reasons for dropping out of school:

24% Disengagement from school
20% Marriage or pregnancy
18% Home and family problems
15% Employment-related problems
8% Social behavior problems
8% Shortcomings of the school
6% Academic problems

The first two items, accounting for 44% of the total, are the same reasons we discussed in Chapter 1: the respondents were ready—or thought they were ready—to get out in the Real World. In fact, the next four reasons might also be related to the same urgency to become independent, an urgency that is prompted in many cases by a dysfunctional family life. Home and family problems may also be the result of teenage rebellion toward the same rules that were acceptable a few years earlier. Likewise, most young people (of the last four decades, at least) who cite employment-related problems as the reason for dropping out of school were working in the first place because they wanted to be independent, not to buy food or help support the family. And, of course, it is socially unacceptable (social behavior problems) to disregard the rules of school that serve children well but often fly in the face of the itching-to-be-an-adult adolescent. Some people might well blame the school (shortcomings of the school) for his or her inability to cope, an inability that, again, could be rooted in an abusive or dysfunctional family.

Only the last reason might indicate a real problem with learning. But, again, many students who don't keep up with homework, who don't do well on tests, who, in fact, have academic problems, have them because they are preoccupied with things other than schoolwork (such as rampant hormones), not because they are incapable of learning. Yes, there are students who have learning disabilities that make academic progress difficult. And we cannot entirely exonerate a school system that uses dated methodologies when research has shown other, more creative teaching techniques to be more effective. But I believe in the philosophy that 95 percent of students can learn 95 percent of the material *if* it is presented in the right way and on the right level. The point here is that you *can learn*. Whether or not you were a good student in high school was dependent on a number of factors. As an adult who is interested in learning, you are already half way there.

So, if you dropped out of high school, you probably dropped out for reasons other than real problems with learning. (If you are, in fact, learning disabled in some way, that still does not mean you are not college material. Shirl Brunell had brain damage in a certain area that made word recognition difficult but learned how to cope with her learning disability and went on to earn a doctorate. Today, we know much more about learning disabilities and how to diagnose and cope with them. Colleges have free tutoring centers for all students and usually a department to help students with special needs.

You *can* learn college-level material. You may have some catching up to do in some academic areas; however, there is no disgrace in that. What you have learned about life will make some aspects of college easier as you spend more time on some of the things kids right out of high school breeze through.

If you have kids at home

College students with children at home and full-time jobs have difficult rows to hoe, yet those students somehow rise to the challenge. It is truly amazing that some of them do so well. My first impulse is to say that it is harder for women because so many women have the responsibility of running their households. But I've had male students who were sharing duties with working wives and holding full-time jobs themselves as well as taking full loads in school.

Of course, the single parents of either sex who work full time and manage to attend college and take care of children alone are real heroes. Some of them have help from their own parents, perhaps with babysitting, and some have financial help from the government or other sources (see Chapter 3), but still they struggle. What they have in common is the deep desire to make better lives for themselves and their children, and with that kind of desire, they will succeed. They go in knowing what the obstacles will be—or at least having some idea. When they are thrown unexpected curves—like having to take courses they hadn't counted on taking, having to buy new car batteries when tuition is due, or having to buy $100 worth of books for one course—they handle it.

Looking back years later, many of these students are amazed that they actually did it. Natalie, a single mother who worked full-time and attended college five years to earn an elementary teaching certificate, told me that she wasn't sure how she did it or whether she could do it again, but at the time there just weren't any options. She said, "When things came up, I did what I had to do to get by. I didn't even think about the possibility of dropping out of school or changing my plans in any way. It was like I had tunnel vision—like I was a racehorse headed for the finish line. I knew I would make it. I knew I would double my salary. I knew I would have summers off with my son when I got a teaching job. Many people talk about the low salaries teachers make and the terrible conditions, but I was thrilled with my job. I hadn't thought about anything else for five years."

How do people like Natalie do it? How do they juggle class work, homework, and jobs and still spend quality time with their children?

One woman told me that when she started school, she decided she would study only during the time she had previously spent watching television. Gail said, "Well, actually I spent a little more time studying than I had spent watching television, like the hours between 4:30 and 6:00 in the morning when the kids were still in bed. I learned that I didn't really need a full eight hours sleep. I spent four years getting just 5 1/2 or six hours sleep a night. And you're talking to a person who was known as the log-head of the family! I used to think my body required eight or nine hours sleep every night. Now that I've finished school and have a job that requires fewer hours than the one I worked during my school years, I still do not sleep eight hours. In fact, I feel groggy if I sleep more than six hours."

Survival tip

Involve your family in your study. Let your children ask you study questions. They will learn, too.

Another woman told me that when she decided to start college, her children were very young. "I studied with them. I read my assignments to them. I answered review questions to them. They didn't understand a word I was saying, but they listened to me and watched me. I would walk around the room, reciting facts about the industrial revolution or something. I would look at them and laugh and raise my eyebrows or grab them up and say, 'Whitney's idea of interchangeable parts revolutionized the factories of America! Isn't that wonderful?' They thought it was a game."

Older children can also participate in Mom's or Dad's study games. In fact, during the first year of college, when many of the courses overlap with high school courses, families can study together. The rules of English that are printed in the high school grammar books are the same rules college students use when writing their papers. High school students can help college-student parents review algebra, geometry, trigonometry, history, political science, and literature.

So there is no need to exclude the family when studying. Sure, there will be times when you must be alone to study, but with a little creativity, you can make the whole family a part of your college experience.

There is another point about tackling college when you have children at home—you provide a positive role model for them. It has become a kind of tradition in America that children surpass their parents in some way. During the Great Depression, very few Americans could even finish high school, but the parents who missed that opportunity were determined their children would graduate from high school. When the next generation graduated from high school, they worked hard to prepare the way for their children to go to college. Sometimes it happened; sometimes it didn't. But the important thing is that parents show children the value of education—education can make a real difference in lifestyle, not to mention the difference it makes in self-esteem. And if Mom or Dad can manage to go to college while raising a family and making all the sacrifices they make as parents, it becomes a more realistic possibility for children. That doesn't mean, of course, that many of them won't wait a few years to actually get serious about college, but when they do, the model you have set for them will pay off.

If you are a supermom

What about the "perfect homemakers," working or non-working, who decide to go to college? They, perhaps, haven't taught their children to help at home, or even to pick up after themselves. Their families are accustomed to on-time meals and clean clothes. Dana Hughes was such a supermom:

"I guess I had the idea that I was showing my love—or maybe, justifying my existence—by picking up their dirty socks and wet towels. I didn't make them do anything. I was June Cleaver in Nikes. My whole life centered on fulfilling my family's needs. When I first decided to start college, my husband was against it, my kids were against it, and I don't think the dog liked the idea either. My husband said that it would be the beginning of the end of our marriage. He thought it would change me. My kids said they would be embarrassed to have a mother in college. They said it was childish—imagine that!

"At first, I thought my husband was right. It was total hell around the house. The only peace I could get was in the school library, and when I came home, everyone started yelling at me at once: 'Where's my clean jeans?,' 'There's nothing in this house to eat,' and 'Don't you love us anymore?' I'm talking about half-grown kids—teenagers —and an able-bodied man who couldn't feed and dress themselves! Finally, the kids started washing their own clothes out of necessity, and my husband went to Wal-Mart and bought himself some clean socks and underwear, but they were all still very unsupportive.

"I was on the verge of dropping out of school when I talked to a woman in one of my classes who had been through something similar. She said she finally sat everyone down and asked for their support and cooperation and together they outlined responsibilities for each family member.

"So I called a family meeting. I started by telling each one of them that I loved him and asking if he loved me and if he loved everyone else in the family. After we had all affirmed that we loved each other, I asked for suggestions for solving our problems—it was like everyone was pulling for himself and to hell with the other guy. They started out by declaring that my decision to go to college was just bad timing because they were so busy at school and work, so we started outlining duties and how much time each one took. Then we made a schedule for the week, with each of us taking a turn at preparing dinner, doing laundry, and cleaning. And we were all responsible for picking up after ourselves. I won't say that everything went without a hitch after that, but it was certainly a lot smoother. And the kids are better for it, I think, because they learned to be responsible to others—not to mention the fact that they learned some valuable survival skills. How can anyone who doesn't even know how to operate a washing machine live in this world?

"The kids are on their own now, and my husband and I have a better relationship. I have a job that is important to me, and at night we talk about things that happen during our days.

I don't think he discussed his work with me in the old days. Maybe he thought it was all above my head or that I wasn't interested in anything except Pabulum and Blue Cheer!"

Dana's story is a success story. She kept her marriage intact and even improved her relationship with her husband. But others do not finish college with intact marriages. Sometimes the change is all the way.

If your kids have left the nest

Although some say that the "Empty Nest Syndrome" is a myth —that parents are more likely to shout for joy than mourn the last phase of parenthood—it is true that when the last child leaves home, it is a time to redefine goals. The part of your time that before was occupied with extra loads of laundry, chauffeuring, cooking regular meals, etc. is now up for grabs. You can do what you choose. You can sit around and worry that the kids can't possibly do without you—that they can't survive on Big Macs and Beanie Weenies and that they will never have clean clothes, or you can kick up your heels and enjoy your freedom. Yes, you are at a turning point in your life. You have decisions to make about the rest of your life, and any such responsibility and potential for dramatic change will bring on a certain amount of stress. Eric Hoffer said, "We can never really be prepared for that which is wholly new. We have to adjust ourselves, and every radical adjustment is a crisis in self-esteem. We undergo a tests; we have to prove ourselves. It needs inordinate self-confidence to face drastic change without inner trembling." It is up to you whether you see the change as the death of an old life or as the birth of a new life. Your children do not need you in the same way they once did, but there are many new challenges to take on—college is only the beginning. You gave child-rearing your best shot (even though you probably made some mistakes since child-rearing is learned through trial and error, through on-the-job training). Imagine what you can do in college with the same dedication. And, yes, you will make mistakes, but the end result will be well worth the effort.

If you have an unsupportive spouse

Many couples, faced with the reality that they need two salaries, work together to help each other through college. Many young couples start their lives together with plans that both will attend college at some point in the marriage. I have talked to women whose non-college-educated husbands were very supportive and proud of their student wives. For some couples, however, college means trouble. Many women told me their husbands, at least at first, did not want them to attend college.

One of the reasons a decision to go to college can be upsetting to a spouse is that it calls for a renegotiation of the marriage "contract." There is a tendency to want to keep the status quo if it is working to one's benefit. If a husband, for instance, is happy with his life and fairly secure in his marriage, his wife's decision to start college can be taken as a signal that she is not happy in their marriage. He may find it hard to understand that she is happy with him but wants to enrich her life—that happiness starts inside and that part of her fulfillment is to achieve her own goals. He may believe that she simply wants to get an education so she can find a good job and leave him. He may even know someone whose wife went to college and divorced him as soon as she graduated. It happens. Perhaps the college experience did not actually cause the breakup. There may have already been an underlying unhappiness or turmoil in the relationship, and college is a place to grow. If one is growing but the spouse is not, the two may grow apart.

Many women do find college helps them build the self-esteem and acquire the work skills necessary to get out in the world and make it on their own. Again, college doesn't cause the breakup in their marriages, but it can certainly contribute to the factors that make a woman independent. A woman who has been told all her life, for instance, that she is incompetent or that she has an IQ two points below plant life will find out in college she is *not* stupid. This discovery may lead to the demise of an already faltering marriage.

A woman who enters college with the purpose of freeing herself from her husband can try to elicit her husband's support on humanitarian or practical grounds. But some women who want to have their marriages and college too— face the challenge of making their husbands understand the college experience will ultimately be good for the marriage. Linda Crowell, who had considered giving up the idea of college because of her husband's lack of support, said she fought for a long time to reconcile her own desire for college with her husband's insecurities. Finally, she took her husband to a restaurant, sat across the table from him, and calmly said, "*You* can't make me happy unless I am happy myself—in fact, no one can *make* someone else happy. Happiness has to come from within, and for me it takes fulfilling my personal goals as well as our goals together. I know I'm asking you to sacrifice some things for me, but I will do the same for you. I need this for *me*, but it does not mean that I don't love you." Linda said that her husband gradually became less insecure and more supportive, and she was able to complete a two-year degree program.

If you have a jealous spouse

If your wife is jealous of the women in your classes, reassure her constantly that you have a goal in mind—to get a degree—and that you love her and are happy with her. You might even get her to sign up for some classes with you. You can study together and make going to class a date. Go out for pizza after class, and talk about the lecture.

If your husband is jealous of the men in your classes, telling him that all the men on campus are homosexuals probably will not work. The solution is in making him feel secure—making him know that Kevin Cosner and Brad Pitt put together couldn't tempt you. (Also, see the above advice. If he won't sign up for classes, at least get him to tour the campus with you and drag him to the next campus theater production and brag about his abilities in front of your college friends and professors.)

If you have retired from your job

I once received a call from a woman who wanted me to speak to a local writer's club. After we had talked for some time, the conversation turned to college. She said, "I started college when I was sixty-five—that was five years ago. I've had to miss several semesters—I broke a hip, and so forth. But my friend told me that I seem like a different person when I'm going to college."

Why do you suppose a seventy-year-old woman would be interested in going to college, and why would she "seem like a different person" while attending classes? First of all, the woman is not dead. Nor is she sitting passively in a rocker waiting to sprout wings and join the angels. She is interested in exploring the world around her, in finding new joys in relations with her fellow humans. She knows that life is learning. She has goals and finds satisfaction in reaching those goals, and when she's in college she feels better because she is learning and growing more and setting and reaching more goals. Of course, others notice it and find her more exciting to be around.

I watched a profile on CNN of Doris Travis, an 88-year-old who was graduating from the University of Oklahoma. She will be taking more courses because, she says, "Education never stops." She also noted that she was "happy." Well, I'll tell you, *I'm happy for her*. As I watched her, I realized that I was smiling—*really* smiling, from the heart. To see an 88-year-old who still sees a future—who moves and thinks and seeks—is tonic for the soul. Afterward I felt like a slug, kind of like one feels at a high school reunion when she realizes that gravity is not impartial—that some folks wear better than others. But Doris Travis did have some things going for her. She had a supportive husband who sat alone while she studied and didn't whine and complain, and she didn't have a houseful of pre-schoolers or a cadre of teenagers with which to contend. Still, she serves as an example to us all.

Retirees who go to college don't have time to worry about the aches and pains that often accompany the senior years. But I don't want to imply that a formal college program is the only way to stay mentally and physically active while learning and growing. I remember a woman in Dallas who still taught aerobatics (yes, stunt flying) at age 76. I didn't want to take lessons from her. From a practical standpoint, I decided the odds were against her—that sooner or later, some part would wear out, and I didn't want to be in a loop-de-loop with her when it did. But I was inspired by her courage, and now I wish I had been more courageous and experienced flying with her. She and Doris offer something to think about when we feel like whining. And think about Georgia Clark, the whitewater rafter who guided thrill-seekers through turbulent water until she was 81 years old. She was both student and teacher of the river. I'll adapt Don Henley's words: You don't stop learning when you get old; you get old when you stop learning.

If you have lost a partner to death or divorce

The loss of a spouse through death or divorce results in traumatic re-adjustment. Married couples grow to depend on each other in so many ways that loss of a spouse can be devastating. Especially for those whose identities were so closely tied to a spouse, it may seem at first that some part of the survivor has died or is gone. We talk about being "part of each other" in a close relationship. But still, no matter how metaphorically we might be bound to another, the fact remains that a *whole* person survives—perhaps one who feels tremendous grief and/or anger but who is *still* a whole person. The tendency to withdraw from others leaves one in a neat position for extensive self-pity, and it can turn into a way of life instead of a natural grieving period.

While it is true that life from then on will not be the same for someone who has lost a mate through death or divorce, there are still joys to be found, new people to meet, and personal growth to be experienced. College is the perfect place to start a new phase in life. The new people, the new ideas, the new goals are therapeutic in many ways. There is a social structure in college for which many married people, especially those with children, do not have time. The theater productions, the special lectures from visiting scholars, the special showings of films, the poetry readings, etc. are all available to adult students who have time to enjoy them. Meeting people who share common interests and people who are interestingly diverse can enrich the life of someone who has just lost a loved one. Don't wait for others to speak first and miss opportunities to make new friends.

Survival Tips

The Home Front

You can't be all things to all people. If the idea of a dirty house makes you crazy, you will probably change—not because you want to but because you must survive. It is impossible to spend all your time tracking dust and keep up your studies. Here are two options:

1. You can adopt the Joan Rivers philosophy of housekeeping: Why bother? You cook. You wash. You clean the toilet. You vacuum. Six months later you have to do it all again!

2. You can learn to manage your time and compromise on the dust tracking. Set aside an hour or two on the weekend to clean. Move through the house like a tornado, and call it clean. You can do the big stuff on spring break and over the Christmas holidays. I'm not advocating slobbery, but a college degree lasts a lot longer than a clean house. If you're afraid you'll lose the knack for cleaning, just think of the post-degree days and making enough money to hire someone to come in once a week to clean—perhaps someone who is working her way through college cleaning houses. (It's a pretty lucrative business, I've heard.) You might cut a few corners on the budget now (forego a night of eating out, etc.) and pay someone to spend three hours cleaning every week.

Enlist the help of family members. Keep reminding them that you love them and show appreciation for the things they do. Making a big deal over one small step (taking out the garbage, for instance) can result in bigger and better things. Even when family members are not being extra supportive, thank them for their support anyway. It worked for Bartles and Jaymes. (Remember the wine cooler commercials?) It might work like a self-fulfilling prophecy; at the least, it will make them feel guilty when they are downright nasty about having to help around the house.

Teenagers

Teenagers might have to be reminded occasionally that you diapered them when you could have been doing other things, but most teens, even though they might not admit it, are proud of parents who go to college.

One thing to consider when teens seem to be very antagonistic about your attending college is that they may actually be worried about you, worried that you can't make it and will be disappointed. Adolescents have a tendency to underestimate their parents in some areas, and college-after-thirty seems to be one of the areas. Teens, spouses, and other loved ones may send negative messages when they are really very concerned. Rather than say they are worried you are getting in over your head, they might try in other ways to discourage you.

Young children

If you have young children, enlist their help, too. Young children love to be helpful, and you'll be doing them a favor if you let them help you. Remind them frequently why you are attending college and that you appreciate their help and their support. Take time out to do special things with them. You may at times have to resort to "quality vs. quantity" time, but they will remember those special events. When you don't have time to cook a real meal, take the sandwiches to the park for an hour-long picnic. Or take your books along and make it an afternoon outing.

When my stepchildren were younger, I took a break from my weekend studies to plop a package of hotdogs and a loaf of bread on the table for lunch. After my husband and the kids looked at me as if I were an alien being, I asked, "Well, whadaya want, candlelight?" I grabbed a couple of candlesticks, lit the candles, and drew the shades. The kids got a kick out of eating hotdogs by candlelight. In fact, they still make "candlelight dinner" jokes.

Jobs

If you are working a low-paying job while attending college, you might consider changing to one that will allow you to use some of your work time for study. There are many jobs that require a warm body more than constant attention. Examples of jobs that have the possibility of free time for study are receptionist jobs, security jobs, night hotel desk clerk jobs, photo stand jobs, etc. Sitting with someone who is in the hospital or home care is another possibility. The best shifts for studying at many jobs are the graveyard shifts (from midnight to morning), and you might find that the abnormal working hours fit in beautifully with your school schedule.

Controlling stress

One way to control stress is to really believe in yourself. Since people aren't born with that ability, it takes a certain amount of effort. In fact, you might need to constantly remind yourself that you are capable of succeeding, that you have what it takes to succeed, and that you are determined to succeed.

Affirmations are statements of belief or, perhaps, statements you would like to believe. If you say every day (or several times a day) that you are healthy in body and in mind and that you are capable of doing what you need to do to reach your goals, you will convince yourself that those statements are true. Of course, they *are* true. You can do anything that is required of you. But sometimes doubt creeps in and self-confidence slips away unless we make conscious efforts to keep the old devil doubt at bay.

Laughter is another way of controlling stress. Sometimes it is necessary to lighten up, to "chill out." Yes, what we are doing is important, but no one (to my knowledge) has actually been institutionalized from making a B instead of an A (although I do know a woman who spent a day in bed over a B) or from making an embarrassing statement to a classmate or an instructor. If you do your best, you have succeeded.

And there is no future in kicking yourself over something that has already happened and cannot be changed. Much of the stress we feel is the result of attitudes about and expectations of ourselves. If you can be perfect and survive, great! But if trying to be perfect costs you your health, your sanity, or your family or causes you to drop out of college, back off!

Feeling inadequate, guilty that you aren't super-mom, super-wife, super-student, super-friend, etc. is counter-productive. Years ago, I heard a friend say very solemnly, "Guilt is the cancer of life." I held on to that statement and admired him for having such a profound thought. Years later, he told me he had stolen the line from Ann Landers. Oh, well. So I misplaced my admiration all those years. But the statement is true. Guilt eats away at the psyche, limiting our ability to enjoy the present. There is simply no future in guilt or remorse.

Forgetting about past blunders is healthy. Focusing on the present is healthy. We have new opportunities every day to prove ourselves. Yes, finishing college is a long-term goal. But the steps you are taking today are important, and they are worth your undivided attention. You simply don't have time to dwell on past errors.

And don't be afraid to ask for help when you need it. Colleges have full-time counselors who have training in stress-management techniques. In fact, many schools offer workshops or seminars in stress management, and you can find self-help books on dealing with stress at the college library. You might also incorporate an aerobics or other exercise class into your schedule for fun and stress relief.

Taking One Step at a Time

Remember the song "High Hopes"? The little ant, by damn, moved that rubber tree plant, and you can, too. Each step you take is a step toward fulfilling your goal. But perhaps more important than the *end* is the *means*—the fun you have in getting there. Enjoy each step as you take it. What you learn and what you experience is part of you; you own it. You might make a little sign to remind yourself of General Patton's famous words, "When the going gets tough, the tough get going." To help yourself "get going," make lists with short-term and long-term goals. When you write down things you have to do—things that make worry worms that gnaw at your mind, you can quit worrying about them and focus on the one thing that must be completed first. Prioritize your lists and mark off each item as you finish the task. You will have evidence that you are accomplishing something, and that evidence serves as motivation for future work. I have even stooped to listing something I had just finished in order to mark it off my list.

You might also mark a calendar with your long- and short-term goals, special events, and Must Remember dates and color-code each category.

Chapter 3
The First Steps

Making a decision to go to college is a big step—one that will be accompanied by feelings of fear, anxiety, and anticipation of hard work and extreme pleasure and self-satisfaction. But you don't have to be ready to start class tomorrow to check out the possibilities in your area.

Since adults are usually settled into a particular region, location is an important factor. Whereas high school seniors might shop around the country for an ideal school and move to the college area, adults usually shop in the neighborhood—perhaps a 60- or 70-mile radius of their homes—and commute to school. In a metropolitan area, you will find many colleges and universities.

You might choose a school on the basis of nearness to your home, but there are several other factors to consider. You might discover that the extra driving time to a less-convenient school will pay off in the availability of course offerings or in the kinds of nontraditional credit given (see CLEP Tests and Occupational Competency Credit). You will probably also consider tuition cost and availability of scholarships before deciding.

Choosing a school

If you live in an area with several colleges and universities, you might start by calling the schools and requesting a catalog, admissions form, financial aid application (if needed), and schedule of classes for the next semester. Find out about the admission requirements. You may get a clerk or student aide when you call, someone who doesn't know the answers to all of your questions. But if you talk to an admissions counselor, be sure to tell him or her that you are over 25 years of age. Most schools have different requirements for students over 25. For instance, younger students might be required to submit high school diplomas, ACT or SAT scores, and entrance exams while older students are admitted immediately or asked to take a general placement exam. The reason for these differences is older students are more likely to do well in school no matter what kind of grades they made in high school. That was a long time ago.

Visit the campuses, and talk to counselors at the schools that interest you. Now, that all sounds simple enough: visit a school. But after reading that, you may have had a physical reaction to the thought of going to a college campus—a queasy feeling in your stomach, perhaps. Taking that first step onto a college campus may take courage. A journalist friend of mine said she drove to a campus and got out of the car, then back in, then out—four times before she finally made it to the administration building. She was afraid, intimidated by the idea of going to college. In a college parking lot, a woman walked up to me and said, "Excuse me. Can you tell me where I should go. I've never been here before. I don't know where to go." I could see fear in her face but also excitement, I think. She was taking a step that could change her life, and that's both scary and exciting. As I walked her to the building, I told her the story about my friend Kathy who got out and back in the car four times, hoping she would find courage in the fact that others had felt the same fear she was feeling.

I will say to you, if you can find a friend to go with you, great! If not, don't let that keep you from making that first move. Remember that the fear of doing something new is temporary, and part of what you are feeling is the excitement of being on the threshold of something new, challenging, and wonderful.

Community colleges

Many metropolitan areas have several community, or junior, colleges and perhaps several branches of the same college. These colleges usually have two-year courses of study and offer associate degrees. Many offer trade, or vocational, courses and degrees in fields such as welding, electronics, cosmetology, etc. in addition to degree programs in the arts and sciences. Many also offer non-credit classes in a wide variety of areas. You might find classes in country dancing, pottery making, foreign languages, doll making, amateur photography, and stress management—to name only a few of the offerings found at many colleges. Whatever your interest, you can probably find a class in it at a community college.

Many people who would not feel comfortable starting at a university will start with a course or two in the continuing education department (perhaps even an exercise course), have a wonderful time, make new friends, and decide to enroll in regular academic courses. The community, or junior, college environment is supportive to adult students, and most schools actually solicit adult participation. The colleges also are experienced in helping adults through the college system and in making adults feel at ease.

Both adults and traditional students often find that they can save money by taking general studies courses, the courses required for graduation from four-year universities, at community colleges. The tuition at community colleges often averages less than half the tuition at universities. And chances are good that you will find the instruction better and easier for basic studies courses.

You may be wondering how the educational level can be better and the course work be easier at the same time. Here's how. At universities, many of the lower level, general studies courses are taught by teaching assistants (TAs), rather than by full professors. Many TAs put a lot into their classes, and most try to do a good job. However, for the most part, they have had no classes in teaching methodology nor prior teaching experience. Now, just because a person has not had courses in methodology does not mean he or she won't be a good teacher. In fact, education courses can be shallow and generally useless, yet there are things to be learned about the techniques of teaching. Much of it is learned through experience. Again, TAs generally have no prior teaching experience.

There are exceptions, of course. I was a TA after I had taught in a public high school. And, on the down side, I know a TA who had prior experience in the public schools and tried to carry that same level and method of instruction into her college classes. An adult student who started in her class said she dropped when the TA told the class they would be doing a lot of grammar work (in a writing class) and they would be writing spelling words five times. Perhaps this TA taught elementary students before—I don't know. I do know that her approach—from what I heard—is inconsistent with what research tells us about teaching writing in college.

Now, in contrast to university TAs, community college instructors more often have doctorates in their fields. Either because they couldn't find university jobs, didn't want to relocate, or didn't want the "publish or perish" pressure that university professors face, these people have chosen to teach at community colleges. They know their subject areas and have teaching experience. When I say the work is often *easier*, it is because of the knowledge and experience of the instructors. To illustrate—try learning statistics from someone who doesn't really know the subject and doesn't know what works best in helping students learn. I have. I signed up for a graduate-level statistics course with a professor who had taught the course for years. He made everything make sense. It was easy. I was making A's in the course until I had to drop it. (I'll tell you more about *why* I had to drop it later.) When I signed up for the evening course the next semester, it was with a psychology professor who was teaching statistics for the first time. He seemed thoroughly confused, and so was I. I still remember the whole class tilting their heads sideways as he wrote around the side of the chalkboard. I made my first C in a graduate course. (Yes, I should have dropped the course early on, but it's not in my nature to drop courses. I really didn't even consider the possibility.)

So, now you know why I say community college courses can be better and easier than university counterparts. This is not always the case; in fact, the reverse is sometimes true. The only way to know about a particular course or instructor is to talk to students who have had the course, evaluate their advice (more on this later), and check out the instructor.

One other point that is worth mentioning—community colleges usually have a higher percentage of adult students, and instructors are accustomed to giving the extra help that many adult students need. And community colleges are likely to be smaller and the people friendlier than their university counterparts. Because the campus is smaller, the classes are usually smaller. Some university classes may have 100 or more students in a class, but community college instructors deal with smaller classes and usually know most of the students in a class by name. Branch campuses of large universities are usually much like community colleges in that they are smaller and offer students more personal attention.

Senior colleges and universities

Universities are usually four-year schools that grant bachelor degrees and offer graduate level coursework. (I say *usually* because some universities offer only junior and senior level courses.) Although most universities offer a standard, or core, curriculum, they differ in specializations. For instance, one school might specialize in programs related to agriculture, while offering other unrelated degrees; another school might specialize in aeronautics or engineering. Universities also vary in their offerings of advanced degrees (master and doctorate degrees).

Private universities are those schools that get the bulk of their support from churches or other institutions. These schools usually are much more expensive than the state-supported universities. Whereas tuition at a state university might run in the hundreds of dollars per semester, tuition at a private school might be in the thousands.

Admission requirements at private institutions are also sometimes higher than those of state-supported schools. Yet, again, students over 25 years of age are usually admitted under requirements different from those of traditional freshmen.

You may choose to enter a four-year university directly or move to one after you have completed two years of study at a community college. Either way, whether you choose a private university or a state university will probably depend on the following factors:

1. Financial resources and/or availability of scholarships
2. Convenience to your home
3. Courses of study offered

The last item, courses of study offered, requires more thought than the other two. While you can readily assess schools on the basis of cost and distance from your home, you will need to study the catalogs from the prospective schools carefully (and maybe get help in interpreting them from a counselor) before you make a decision based on courses offered. The first thing you want to know is whether or not the school is accredited. Most schools are accredited, but there are "fly by night" institutions around the country that are set up to take students' money and give them little in return like some of those advertised on television may be. Also, if a school is not accredited, you may not be able to transfer your course work to another institution.

The distance you must travel to attend classes and your work and family schedule may also be factors in your pre-enrollment decisions. For instance, if you must commute several miles to school or if you have work and family obligations that dictate the amount of time you can spend in class, you might want to spend a couple of months studying before you take placement exams. The time you spend studying will help ensure that you will go right into regular classes; consequently, every hour you spend in class will count toward your degree.

For example, Janet was thirty-something when she decided to start college. She was divorced, and her only child was in high school. Her job as a police dispatcher in a small town allowed her to use some work time for study. Since she lived sixty miles from the nearest university, she was determined to get as much out-of-class credit as she could. She needed a higher-paying job and was determined to complete her degree as quickly as possible. She listed from the catalog the courses she needed for the degree she had chosen (sociology). She then checked the CLEP tests and correspondence courses that would fit her plan. As she worked her way through the correspondence courses, she signed up for and studied for two CLEP tests per month. In less than six months, she had earned 29 hours of CLEP credit and 12 hours of correspondence credit. She had actually completed more than a year's work. She had completed most of the general study courses and earned elective credit. She had not taken any math courses, however, so before she took the math placement exam required for on-campus classes, she studied a basic math book. When she started attending classes, she planned her schedule carefully to get the most from each trip to the university. She earned a four-year degree in just over two years. To say this wasn't easy is probably an understatement, but Janet was willing to make the sacrifices necessary to finish school in a hurry. If you are like Janet, you will certainly want to take advantage of any nontraditional credit you can get. (See CLEP tests and other nontraditional credit.)

If, on the other hand, you plan to take a more leisurely pace with your studies, you might elect to take developmental courses, whether or not you are required to, instead of doing a self-paced review. You might take courses you think will be fun instead of focusing on required courses. Instead of taking a full load, you might only take one or two courses each term. For example, Martha Thompson already has her own business, and she doesn't want a new career. She does want a college degree, but she isn't in a hurry. She takes a couple of classes each semester and enjoys every moment of class time and study time. She says that she plans to go to school for the rest of her life because school "keeps her motivated."

You probably, like most adult students, fall somewhere between the two extremes mentioned above. Adults who enroll in college usually set realistic goals for themselves, realizing they do have families and jobs to deal with, and they need some time for themselves, too. Too fast a pace can cause burnout for some people. They become exhausted and don't feel they are doing justice to any of their many roles. Other people seem to thrive on the pace, the constant deadlines, and maintain their enthusiasm from day one until graduation. The important thing is you know yourself better than anyone else, and you know your responsibilities. Take it easy, at first, anyway.

Most people have a tendency to underrate their capabilities where college is concerned. But you will find out as you go exactly how many courses you can handle in one term. That doesn't mean you won't be thrown a curve once in awhile (a course that requires more of your time and energy than you had anticipated). And sometimes situations outside school can serve as unexpected drains—illness of a child or spouse or parent, perhaps. Some students find it necessary to drop out for a semester because of a family crisis or even a job-related crisis. If that happens to you, remember that you have worked too hard to give up permanently.

If you have a crisis to deal with near the end of a semester that causes you to drop out temporarily, talk to instructors about taking an *I*, or *Incomplete*, or an *X*. You may be able to make up the work during the first part of the next semester. Remember, though, that you will be allowed only a certain amount of time to finish the work. If you do not complete the work in the time allowed, the *I* or *X* will turn into an *F*, and you will have to repeat the entire course to replace the F. At any rate, don't simply leave school without withdrawing or making arrangements with instructors. If you do, your instructors will have no option other than giving you F's in your courses, and it's not hard to figure out what F's do to grade point averages (GPA's).

If you have to drop out temporarily, you may find it hard to get back the momentum you had when you first started. But usually adults are anxious to get back in class and continue the process of reaching the goal, to get back in the stimulating environment of college, and to get back the fellowship of other students.

Admission

When you ask for an admission packet, you will find out exactly what you need to give the school. Admission procedures should be handled before registering for classes. You might need to send off for some documents and wait for them to arrive in the mail or be sent to the school. You might be asked to supply a transcript from your high school, which will mean writing to the high school and asking that a copy of your transcript be sent to the college or university. You might be asked to supply some kind of health certificate or statement from a medical doctor. You will probably be asked to talk to an academic advisor prior to registration. Doing this ahead of time will reduce the frustration involved in registration when hundreds of people are trying to do the same thing at the same time. On registration day, you will sign up for the specific courses you choose. You can avoid the rush by taking advantage of early registration.

Financial aid

Although financial aid programs have been tightened up somewhat in the past few years, there are still government programs available and a variety of scholarship programs that are available through schools and through civic and church organizations. Most schools have a financial aid office to handle questions and process applications.

If you plan to apply for financial aid, you will need to begin the process by filling out an application months before you plan to start school. Colleges have application packets for grants and loans. You will need your current income tax forms and may need to call or write letters for other information. The process of filling out the application is tedious, but not hard. You may, however, want to get help to make sure you haven't missed anything on the form. If one little thing is missing, your application can be delayed (and consequently, your money for the semester). There are strict deadlines for submitting applications.

There is a number to call for information on federal aid: 1-800-333-INFO. Also, legislation has been introduced that will allow more adults to qualify for government grants and loans. Before, owning your own home could make you ineligible, but the laws are changing. So, don't take the advice of someone who knew the old rules; check with the financial aid office to find out current laws. (Don't forget that loans are expensive. You can get deferments on repayment until you graduate, but that means filling out forms every semester. You don't want to let a student loan go into default. You may have heard about all the doctors, etc. who didn't repay student loans. Well, the doctors may still get by with it since they are self-employed, but everyone else must pay or the IRS will garnish your wages and take any tax refund you have coming.)

If you can't afford to go ahead and enroll for classes before you get help, you may be able to start preparing yourself for regular course work in the school's adult education department—free of charge. Some colleges have a program to loan you money on, perhaps, a three-month pay-back with little or no interest. You could take one or two classes to get started and pay as you go. If you are not eligible for government or state financial aid but need help financing college, check out the scholarships available in your area. *The Scholarship Book* (Prentice Hall) contains a listing of more scholarships than you can imagine—scholarships that are specific to certain people (daughters of coal miners, green-eyed great-grandsons of Civil War soldiers, etc.). Scholarships may be based on where you live, what your interests are, your heritage, whether or not you or your parents were in a union or worked for a particular corporation, etc. Yes, some work is involved in finding available scholarships, but it is worth the effort if you need financial help. You may also be eligible for tuition reimbursement from your employer. Scholarship money sometimes goes unclaimed because many people think they are not eligible and, therefore, don't apply for it. You don't have to be dirt poor or a genius to get a scholarship. You can also find information on the Internet by beginning with a general search for "college scholarships." Although websites change, you can also try "finaid," "fastweb," and "fresch" (preceded by www. And followed by .com).

Placement tests

Don't be frightened of placement tests. If you were fairly good at math and English in high school but feel that you've forgotten much of it, use the review chapters in this book to get a general idea of how much help you will need. If you answer most of the questions or even know that you once knew the answers to most of the questions, you will probably be able to brush up on your own. Study the information before you take the placement exam at the college of your choice. Of course, I can't guarantee that if you know the information in these sections you will not be asked to take developmental courses, but you should feel much better about taking the test.

If the material seems completely new to you, you will probably want to take the developmental courses that colleges and many state universities offer. (See Developmental Courses below.)

GED classes

Many community colleges offer free tutoring to adults, especially to those who need to obtain GEDs before starting regular classes. If you don't have a high school diploma or

GED, you will probably be required to take and pass the GED test before enrolling in regular classes. This is a good requirement. There is nothing worse than being stuck in a situation for which you are not prepared. I had a student once in a developmental course who had a third-grade reading level. He had slipped through the cracks; he had gotten around the rule that requires one to have a high school diploma or GED to take college courses. He tried very hard, and he made much progress. But it was embarrassing for him to know he was so far behind the other students, and he ended up dropping out. Had he first worked through GED classes with tutors, he would have been better prepared to start even the remedial classes.

Choosing classes

If you do plan to start at a two-year college and transfer to a four-year college, you need to study the general requirements of the four-year university of your choice. You can usually find out from the college which courses will transfer to a university for credit in an equivalent course, but you might want to double check with the university before you sign up. This warning is not meant to imply that a college would intentionally steer you wrong, but accidents do happen. For instance, a student might be assured that a business math course at a college will transfer as one of the general studies math courses only to find out later at a university that business math will only transfer as an elective and that another course in algebra or geometry is required.

But, if you start to feel overwhelmed by all the possibilities, you can take a safe route the first semester by taking only those courses that you are absolutely sure will transfer. For instance, you might sign up for freshman English and college algebra. Or you might choose freshman English and a history course. (I included freshman English both times because it is very important that you polish your writing skills early in your college career.) By the end of the first semester, you will have a better feel for working your way through the catalogs or getting specific course information. Do not be discouraged by the complexity of course descriptions in the catalogs. The descriptions may have been written by people who wanted to make their courses sound important in order to justify their existence.

Also, if you have a special interest or already know what your major area of study will be, try to include a course from that area each semester. If you love art, for instance, and want to major in art, taking an art course at the same time you are taking your first English or math course will help ensure that you *enjoy* your college experience.

Developmental courses

As mentioned earlier, both colleges and universities usually have different admission requirements for students over 25 years of age. Many schools do, however, require that all students take some kind of placement exam. This exam is not for the purpose of giving or denying admission. It is to determine whether or not the student needs developmental (sometimes called *remedial* or *basic* or *preparatory*) help before taking some of the required courses—especially English and math courses. Some states require that students pass a test later, before they have completed a certain number of hours of course work. But colleges in even those states will usually require an initial placement exam to ensure that students will enroll only in courses in which they have a reasonable chance of succeeding.

If you are worried about taking a placement exam, the reviews in chapters 7, 8, 10, and 11 will help you prepare. You may be able to study the chapters and go right into regular classes. If, however, the school asks you to take developmental courses, do not feel embarrassed about it. One of my students told me she wasn't upset that she had to take a remedial math course; she was relieved that the course was offered. That attitude toward remedial course work is healthy. One woman said she refused to take a remedial math course that would not count toward her degree and realized later the course would have made College Algebra much easier and less stressful. She found herself spending more hours in the tutoring center just to pass College Algebra than she would have spent in the remedial course. You can avoid the stress of going into a class you are not prepared to take by getting the help you need beforehand. The developmental, or remedial, classes are noncredit; they do not count in your grade point average or toward degree requirements, but don't think of the time spent in such a course as wasted time.

Also, most schools have writing, reading, and math centers to help prepare students for regular class work. In these centers, you can get one-on-one tutoring, watch videotapes or listen to audio tapes about the subject, do practice exercises and activities, and get study guides and related hand-outs—and it's free.

If you are asked to take developmental courses, make sure you get a good grasp of the subject area. If you happen to end up with a poor instructor, supplement the course with time in the school's writing center or math lab where tutors will help you. Even if you have good instructors for these courses, you may need additional help from tutors. It is important that you develop writing and math skills early, not only for future English and math courses but also for courses in other subject areas. For instance, you will probably be asked to write papers in any number of classes, and knowledge of the subject can get lost in a paper that is poorly written. In the same way, a basic foundation in math will help you in future science, accounting, and economics courses.

You don't have to have a specific major in mind to start course work. Although there is always a chance that particular courses will not fit into your degree plan once you decide on a major area of study, the courses can usually be used as electives (See the Glossary). A counselor can help you plan your coursework; however, you should be familiar with the catalog yourself, particularly if you plan to transfer from a community college to a university. Counselors will not intentionally steer you wrong, but remember that it is a business and his/her job is to recruit you. Be sure to ask whether each course transfers to the university you plan to attend.

Note: If a course is listed in the catalog as having a prerequisite course, another course that should be taken prior to taking the listed course, make sure you take the courses in the correct order, or talk to the instructor to find out whether you have the skills needed to succeed in the course.

General studies courses

After you have chosen a college and have the admission process underway, study the catalog sections on General Studies, the required courses for most degrees. Although some colleges offer trade or vocational degrees that do not require a full sequence of general study courses, most degree programs will require some variation of the following courses:

Two to four English courses

Usually, the first two courses focus on writing skills. The first writing course will be designed to teach you the different kinds of writing. For instance, you might be asked to write papers comparing one object or concept to another; describing in detail a person, object, or idea; describing a process of doing something, etc. The course may focus on personal writing and the kind of writing you can do from your own knowledge. (See Chapter 7.)

Second courses might have one of two focuses: literary analysis or argumentation. Courses that focus on the interpretation and analysis of literature (not as hard as it sounds) use stories and poems to teach students critical reading and thinking skills. Courses that focus on argumentation also teach critical reading and analysis, but the material analyzed, instead of literature, might be political speeches, advertising, editorials, etc. I teach the second course in the argumentation format. Although the course might be the most difficult course many students will take, I find that both younger and older students thoroughly enjoy the class and take great pride in the discoveries they make. And I think students leave the class with a more critical eye toward the blitz of information that is thrown at them daily.

Another important aspect of the second course is the research process. Whether the course focuses on literary analysis or argumentation, a research paper will probably be required. The difference will be in the topic of the research paper. Literary analysis classes usually require a literary research paper; the topics for research papers in argumentation classes are varied, usually depending on students' interests. The objectives are, in part, for students to learn to use the library to find source material for their papers and to learn to document the material they include in their papers (see Chapter 9).

Note: If you enroll at a school in which the "multicultural craze" has permeated the English department, you may have to learn writing skills elsewhere. Many schools have given in to factions demanding multicultural reading courses in lieu of Freshman Composition. In these classes, you might read the works of women poets, for instance, yet not get the real help you need with writing. Some folks who advocate this kind of course as a replacement for traditional Freshman English courses may be using the legitimate need to introduce students to a wide variety of writers as an excuse to avoid doing a difficult job—teaching writing. It is much harder to teach students to write than it is to discuss literature. Again, if you find yourself in a freshman composition class that isn't really a freshman composition class, use either a traditional composition textbook, lots of practice, and help from the writing center to learn writing skills, or take freshman composition at another school.

Third and fourth English courses are usually literature courses. Some schools offer Introduction to Literature courses that provide a survey of fiction, poetry, and drama. Other schools require courses in American, British, or World literature or any number of approaches such as courses in the modern novel, film, women's studies, ethnic literature, etc. Some schools allow other humanities courses—art history, for example—as substitutes.

Two math courses

These courses might be fundamentals of math courses that include a sampling of algebra, geometry, trigonometry, etc., or they might be courses in two specific math areas, depending on your major area. Some degree plans require specific courses.

Math courses require a great deal of study time, especially if you were not a math whiz in high school, and usually include a great deal of homework. The new high school graduates are accustomed to thinking math, and they know math language. If, like many adults, you depend on a calculator to do your computing, you may have to shift gears to get into math mode. Until you feel comfortable with your math skills, you will probably want to limit the number of additional courses you take when you are taking math courses. And don't forget the free help from math labs.

History courses

A traditional arrangement is a first course in the history of the United States through the Civil War and a second course that deals with the Reconstruction period after the Civil War through the present. Some states require a course in that state's history for teaching certification. Other programs might include world history of different periods.

You will probably be required to write two or three papers during the semester in each history class. And you may want to use a tape recorder (with the teacher's permission) until you find out the priorities of each instructor. Some instructors may be obsessed with dates or may include material on tests that is not in the textbook but that was covered in class. Other instructors may be more concerned with periods in history, with making sure students understand the social and cultural environments of the periods. After the first test in a class, you will be able to make a better assessment of the instructor's focus. You will probably want to attend the first class before you buy a book. Some instructors test from their lectures, not the textbook. You may be able to buy an old edition history text and save a lot of money.

Political science courses

Some states require a course in state government in addition to a traditional political science course. Other states might require the state government course only for certain degrees. You may be required to write papers in these classes. You may also find that you change your television viewing habits while enrolled in political science, or government, courses. For instance, instead of watching reruns of *Cheers*, you may turn over to CSPAN or watch Brit Hume on *FoxNews* and *Crossfire* and *Evans and Novak* on CNN and *Hardball* on CNBC. And you will probably read *Newsweek* instead of *People* or *Redbook*. You might want to keep a journal, recording the interesting bits of information that you hear or read for future papers or tests.

Science courses

These courses involve laboratory work and may be in biology, zoology, geology, oceanography, etc., depending on the student's interest or major area of study. The lab time for some courses might be almost equal to the time required for a separate, complete course. Science teachers tend to think the stuff is easy, but be prepared to dig. Some science labs do not even follow the course text. You may have two sets of information, tests, etc. And often these courses, especially the labs, are taught by TAs who may be either power crazed or wonderful.

A science lab usually accounts for one-fourth of the course grade and can make or break your grade. If the course is especially hard, you may be able to bring up a low grade with your lab credit.

Social Science courses

Courses in sociology, psychology, social work, or counseling might be included as options. These classes usually involve more in-class discussion than homework, but you will probably be required to write papers, take tests, memorize terms, and, perhaps, do some research. You will probably enjoy these courses, no matter how hard you work.

Physical Education courses

Requirements are different at some schools for students who are over 25 years of age. You may get by with fewer courses than is required of traditional freshmen, but still you will probably have to take at least two courses. Most schools offer a wide range of PE courses such as bowling, scuba diving, tennis, aerobics, etc. If you are worried about getting killed in a high-impact aerobics class, ask about beginner courses. You may feel more comfortable in an evening class, which will probably have a higher percentage of adult students.

Most of the general studies courses can be taken at community colleges and transferred to universities, but it is smart to make sure any course you take will transfer if your ultimate goal is to get a four-year degree. If you decide to pick up an associate degree at a community college before you start on a bachelor's degree, you may be required to take courses that will not transfer to a university general studies program, but, again, you will need a certain number of elective courses and may be able to fit these courses into your degree plan.

Note: Although you may not be required to take a computer course, you may choose to take at least an introductory class. Be advised that these courses often require hours of computer lab work to complete assignments with no additional credit. If you don't know how to use a word-processing program, you certainly need to know that. But you may be able to learn that in the school's writing center. Unless you plan to make a career of computer science, you may want to avoid computer programming courses. Whiz kids who write programs are everywhere; those of us who are not computer whiz kids simply buy their programs and use them.

Nontraditional credit

CLEP tests

Do you remember the television ads depicting Abraham Lincoln in an employment office? The personnel officer asked Lincoln about his education and his skills, and Lincoln's responses didn't seem very promising. The gist of the message was that what you have learned in adult life and in the work world is worth something. The College Level Examination Program (CLEP) tests were designed to give people college credit—a kind of head start—for their knowledge. However, the tests are specific and most require some kind of content area study. If you decide to try for CLEP credit, the *Guide to CLEP Examinations* is the best investment you can make. You can order the book from College Board Publications, Box 886, New York, NY 10101-0886. Check the website (www.collegeboard.com) for the current price. The guide lists books to study and has sample questions and explanations for the different tests. From the guide, you can get a general idea whether or not you want to pursue CLEP credit in a certain area. You are risking the cost of the test. You are allowed to retake the test once after a waiting period of six months.

I don't want to give the idea here that CLEP tests are easy; they require concentrated preparation. Some folks do better on this type of test than others. If you can sit for hours and study independently, you may be able to take advantage of CLEP tests.

Departmental exams

Some schools offer departmental exams in specific subjects. To find out about these tests, read in the general catalog about occupational or departmental credit. For instance, if you have been a secretary for years and are a very good typist, you might be able to get credit for typing by taking a one-time test. Although you might not need a typing course on your transcript to prove your skills, you can use the credit as elective credit. Ultimately, you save time and money for any credit you can pick up through examination. Some schools offer credit for trade or vocational knowledge— printing or agriculture knowledge or management experience. It doesn't cost anything to check out the possibility of getting credit for what you know, and you could save big bucks if, for you, time is money.

Correspondence courses

Taking correspondence courses allows you to do most of the work in your living room. You complete assignments on a regular schedule, mail them in, and when you have finished, take a final exam on the material covered. The system works well for those who are well-disciplined and can stick to an independent study schedule; other people need the classroom environment as a constant source of motivation. From my experience with correspondence courses, I believe that much more work is required than is required in on-campus courses. In a classroom, the professor can verify that you have been exposed to a certain amount of material. With correspondence courses, the only way to verify that is through your written exercises and activities. MANY people who enroll in correspondence courses never finish them. Again, it takes a certain personality to work successfully with correspondence courses.

Also, the difficulty of the subject should be a consideration. For instance, if you have had very little math, you would probably be better off taking a course on campus than trying to wade through the material on your own—unless you happen to have a tutor nearby.

Television courses/Distance learning

Television courses offer the convenience of correspondence courses and the help of classroom lectures. Since the programs are aired on a regular basis, there is a built-in motivation to keep up and finish in a certain time period. The drawback is that, like other correspondence courses, the instructor can only judge your knowledge of the material through your written work, and you will probably do more writing than you would in a classroom. Again, it takes self-motivation to complete television course work. Universities often offer distance-learning courses at off-campus sites such as community colleges. The advantage is in taking both upper-level and lower-level courses at the same location.

Continuing education/Non-credit courses

In addition to the developmental courses that do not count toward the hours needed for a degree, most schools offer a series of non-credit courses that are for any and all members of the community.

You might find these courses listed in a separate catalog, so call the continuing education department for a catalog even if you aren't sure whether or not you are interested. You may become interested when you see the variety of courses listed. In fact, many people have their first college experience in one of the continuing education courses. You might find courses in everything from aerobic exercise to weaving. Or, you might find a course in stress reduction to help you through your regular credit courses.

People who have never been to college and don't really have the desire to go, at least, at a particular time in their lives, can sign up for courses that are both fun and informative. The general idea, especially at community colleges, is that people never stop learning. They may have different needs and interests at different times in their lives, and colleges are created to service these needs and interests.

Getting through the bureaucracy

Schools are bureaucracies. They are full of clerks, some of whom are ducks and some of whom are eagles. Schools have many competent, well-informed professionals. It is possible that your first encounter will be with someone who is very competent and helpful. It is also possible that you will reach someone, a student worker perhaps, who is working her first day at the job and knows as much about what she's doing as my Aunt Matilda did right before the white coats locked her away. My point is don't trust the information you get from someone if it (1) doesn't sound right or (2) isn't what you wanted to hear. Remember, the rules were made for 18-year-olds, mostly to make it easier on the rulers. You may come in contact with people who simply don't want to put forth the effort it takes to find answers or to make the irrational rational. If that happens, get a second opinion.

To illustrate that point, I'll tell you a story. A woman I'll call Jean decided to go to college in her mid-30s. She had dropped out of high school to get married but was widely read and very intelligent. She had made good grades in English in high school, so she studied for the CLEP test equivalent of the first semester freshman English course. She felt good about it and decided that she was ready to attend classes—although she had not yet received the score on her English CLEP test. I went with her to what was then a local branch of a junior college that was based in a neighboring community. She asked to sign up for the second-semester freshman English class.

The clerk's response: "*I* can't let you sign up for the second semester course until you've had the first course."

I explained to the clerk that Jean had taken the CLEP test and was sure she had passed it.

The clerk's response: "Well, she can't sign up for the second semester course until she's had the first semester course. What's a CLEP test, anyway? I don't know if we accept CLEP tests."

My response: "What do you mean, you don't know if you accept CLEP tests?! *Harvard* accepts CLEP tests!" (Actually, I didn't know that for sure.) "You're telling her she can't sign up for a course, and you don't even know what a CLEP test is?!"

Jean's (embarrassed) response: "That's okay. I'll just wait until next semester to start school."

My response: "No, we'll just have to find someone who knows something, and obviously we won't find that person here. But we *will* come back!"

In spite of Jean's protests not to bother, I drove to the main campus in the neighboring town. I found the English department chairperson at a registration table and stood in line to see her. After I explained the situation to her, she quickly scribbled a note to the clerk to allow Jean to register for the course.

I'm not suggesting that only clerks are capable of bad behavior; in fact, some people would view my behavior in this situation as reactionary, to say the least. But what we have here is a case of "clerk mentality," an unwillingness to look beyond the rules and use reason. These are the people who will readily tell you that you *can't* when they *don't know* whether you can or not, and they won't expend effort to find out. In some situations, persistence pays off. You can keep trying until you find a person who is willing to listen to reason. (This may involve walking across the campus several times.)

But highly paid professionals may also have that restricted view—a view that is common in bureaucracies. Don't be discouraged, though. If you keep trying, you will find someone who, if not able to change the situation, will at least give you a valid reason why it can't be changed.

Now, there are departments that have little flexibility as far as rules are concerned. I'm thinking of the teacher certification office. Many of the rules are legislated by the state, and being a rebel probably won't help. These folks can and will keep you from your immediate goals. My teaching certificate was delayed a semester because of a rule that said three recommendation letters must be on file before one can begin practice teaching. I received a checklist from the certification office that indicated that the three letters were in (professors must send them to the office). But when I tried to register for the practice teaching courses, I was told that one professor had not sent in his letter, and I could not register. I argued that practice teaching didn't actually start for six weeks and that I could get the letter in that time. (It was Saturday, the last day for registration, and the professor I needed was not on campus.) Anyway, to make a long story short, I pointed out the mistake the office had made and threw quite a fit, but I did not register for practice teaching. Others at the same school had threatened class action suits against the certification office. Evidently, incompetency was rampant. And yes, a clerk *can* win out.

I'll tell you of another experience. I mentioned earlier that I was enrolled in a statistics course with a knowledgeable professor but had to drop the course. I had to drop the course because I was forced to do so by the graduate dean. I had registered for three courses during a summer semester. The previous semester, while teaching in a high school full time, I had taken five graduate courses. That was insane, but I knew I could handle three courses during a summer semester when all I had to do was study. However, there was a rule about taking extra courses, a rule I had ignored before. But this time, someone in the graduate office noticed, and I was called in to explain myself. Well, actually I was called in to explain why I had been presumptuous enough to sign up for an overload without first getting the dean's permission. I explained why I knew I could handle the three courses, but that did not matter. I had not gone through proper channels, and the dean had the power. So, my advice here is to get permission from the right person when you want to break a rule. Rules can be broken, but some people are very territorial about their power to break them. Still, don't give up easily if you want to circumvent a rule.

One woman told me that after a couple of years of school, she realized "all the hoops you have to jump through are part of earning a degree—a required course in tolerance and endurance. You must learn to play the game. I felt I had grown a lot when I learned to accept administrative b.s. as just part of the process."

Now, I'll tell you about another experience, a positive experience. When I was an undergraduate student, I needed an advanced composition course for teacher's certification. The course was not offered in the evenings, and I finally had to sign up for a graduate level course to replace it. After I had done that, I decided that other people might be in the same situation, so I called the professor who taught the advanced composition course and told her about my scheduling difficulties and that I felt that I could have passed a test on the course. I also told her that others might be in similar situations. She proceeded to make an advanced placement test available, and another woman passed it immediately. I don't know how many others have taken the test, but I appreciate this professor's willingness to work with students.

Counselors

Most professional counselors are both well qualified and caring. But at registration time, they may be too busy to give you in-depth explanations. Also, at registration time, faculty members from different departments are pulled in to help students through the process. Although the faculty members may be wonderful teachers and be knowledgeable in their content areas, they may not know much about the school catalog. In a sophomore English course I taught at a university, I had a student who had been out of school for eight years and had never had a college-level English course. He had escaped the placement test because he had transfer credit from eight years ago. When he came to me with his concern that he wasn't ready for this course, I asked him how he had done in his freshman-level courses. "Oh, I haven't had that course. The advisor said it didn't matter." It may not have mattered if the student had been a competent writer. But he knew better than anyone else that he wasn't, that he needed help with his writing skills.

Another student told me that she was advised to enroll in Management Information Systems (MIS) and Accounting 221 during the same semester. On the first day of the MIS class, the instructor asked, "How many are concurrently enrolled in Accounting 221?" Then she told the class that it would be virtually impossible to keep up in both classes and do well in them.

Still, you can get good advice from counselors and other advisors. The advice here is to also use other sources of information and read the college catalog for yourself.

Degree plans

A degree plan is like a contract that outlines your course of study and protects you against changes in requirements. Probably someone in your major department will make your degree plan. But you must seek out this information and make an appointment to have the degree plan completed. What if you have no idea what your major will be? Many people are not sure during the first year what they want to choose as a major course of study or even what's available.

If you start at a community college, you will be asked whether you plan to transfer to a university. If you plan to transfer and get a four-year degree, you will probably have a degree plan made for Arts and Sciences, a program that includes the basic general studies courses most universities require. In order to get an associate degree, a two-year degree, you may have to take some courses that will not count toward your bachelor's degree. This is something you will want to check on and decide whether you want the two-year degree as a kind of stepping stone that provides a sense of accomplishment or whether you want just the courses that will transfer to get your bachelor's as soon as possible.

At any rate, when you transfer to a university, you will have to have a new degree plan made. You may not have to do it immediately, but it is to your advantage to have one made as soon as you decide on a major. For example, say you think you want to be a science teacher, but you're not sure. So you dilly around and procrastinate about getting a degree plan. While you are dillying, the catalog is changed, and two more courses are added to the science teacher program. You are stuck with having to take the two additional courses. Now, if you had gotten a degree plan made before the change, you wouldn't have to take the additional courses. And having a degree plan made doesn't lock you in forever. You still have the option of changing your mind and pursuing another major. Some people change degree plans like they change underwear, but at least they have something on file. And having a degree plan can make registration easier. Some schools require that you go through academic advisement every semester unless you have a degree plan.

Nontraditional student organizations

Non-traditional student organizations are groups of adult students who meet and share ideas, problems, and information. Call the student activity office to find out whether there is such an organization at the school you plan to attend or are currently attending. The meetings offer you a chance to meet other adult students and perhaps even involve your family in meetings or social functions. The organizations offer support and encouragement and share strategies for success. Some organizations even keep food banks for adult students who are temporarily in dire straights. If your school doesn't have such an organization, you might consider rounding up some adult students and starting one. The college will probably be very supportive in helping you get organized.

To start your Internet search for nontraditional student organizations and information, check www.antshe.org and www.adulted.about.com.

Survival tip: College terms

AAS: Associate of Arts and Sciences--two-year degrees offered by community and junior colleges. The degree requires the general studies courses that are required for most four-year degrees.

BA: Bachelor of Arts—four-year degree in one of the humanities offered by universities. Requirements usually include a foreign language course of study.

BS: Bachelor of Sciences--four-year degree in one of the sciences offered by universities. (You must know that the irreverent say it goes like this: BS = bullshit; MS = more shit; and PhD = piled higher and deeper.)

MA: Master of Arts--graduate degree that requires approximately two years of study. Again, the requirements are different from the MS.

MS: Master of Science—graduate degree that requires approximately two years of study.

EdD: Doctor of Education—graduate degree that requires approximately eight years of study. Most are granted from the College of Education, a department within the university.

PhD: Doctor of Philosophy—graduate degree that requires approximately eight years of study.

Major: Primary course of study. Usually involves from eight to twelve courses in a subject area.

Minor: Secondary course of study. Usually involves from six to eight courses in a subject area.

Electives: Courses outside the major and minor areas.

General studies courses: Courses that include introductory courses in a variety of subject areas and that may be required for any degree program at a university. General studies requirements, however, vary from school to school.

GPA: Grade point average.

Lower-level courses: Freshman- and sophomore-level courses. A course numbering system will be outlined in the catalog of your school. For example, all freshman-level courses might be preceded with a 1; sophomore courses preceded with 2, and so on.

Upper-level courses: Junior- and senior-level courses.

Graduate courses: Advanced courses that apply to master's degrees or doctorates.

Semester hour: Number of class hours per week.

Chapter 4
What to Expect

Registration

After you have been admitted to the school, you will need to register for classes. There is a specific time period set aside for registration, although some schools allow "pre-registration," or early registration, for those who want to avoid the crowds. Yes, registration day draws a crowd. And, as I mentioned earlier, instructors who might not be completely familiar with the courses in their own departments, let alone the courses of other departments, are called in to help advise students and get them into the proper classes. Because of the rush of registration and the chance you might get someone who is not a professional counselor, you might want to find out if you can pre-register, or at least talk to a counselor before the registration period about the best course choices for you.

Some people wait until registration to begin the admission process, and if you decided at a late date to start college, go ahead. Don't wait until the next semester when you could start achieving your goal now. On the other hand, any head start you can get on the process will cut down on the number of lines you must stand in and the level of frustration. Registration days can be trying for all involved. Hundreds— maybe thousands—of students are all trying to do the same thing at the same time. And no one is crazy about standing in line. It took me several semesters of losing my patience and stomping from building to building to get this form or that form or this signature or that signature to get smart and pre-register. I do, however, have good memories of the days when registration was done with computer cards, when I ran from table to table, collecting cards for the courses I wanted before they filled up and closed.

That brings us to another important aspect of registration: Some courses have limited enrollment. If you have your heart set on a particular course at a particular time with a particular instructor, pre-register. Other people have the same idea. (See Choosing Instructors below.)

It is also good to keep your ears open at registration. You can find out about instructors (who is good, who is not; who is reasonable, who is not; who makes class interesting, who would make a better sleeping pill than instructor, etc.). You can find out about special programs the campus offers. You can find out about the best book buys on and off campus. You can also find out about people. You will see excited students of all ages.

You will also see fear in the eyes of students of all ages. Even though you might hear some 18-year-olds grumble about the courses they "have to take," keep in mind that grumbling is often a defense: They are nervous, too, because they are starting a new period in their lives. If you'll remember your own feelings (or those expressed by your children) when starting first grade, when entering junior high, and when entering high school, you will probably remember periods of high anxiety. Even though starting a new stage in life is exciting, there are unknown elements that cause fear, or at least, hesitation. People have different ways of coping with these fears. Ninth graders on the first day of school might try to appear tough. They're in high school now, and they try to act grown-up even though those little stomachs are quivering. They may feel so nervous that they actually hurt physically.

A good way to handle your own fear is to reach out to others and to focus on making someone else feel better—even if all you can do is say a quick prayer for him or her. You might also make jokes and be especially compassionate with the registration clerks who help you do your forms. They will be more willing to help you if you are nice to them.

Also, it is good to have a friend with you when you take those important steps toward reaching your goal. You may have started working on a friend when you first started thinking about college, perhaps persuading him or her to join you in the college adventure. If you have a friend who is even remotely interested and can be dragged along to registration, take that friend. It is comforting to know that you have that support. It is also comforting to know someone on campus. You may even talk a friend into signing up for the same classes. Although each of you might have to make some compromises on choices, the two of you will help each other through those first enrollment steps and, if possible, through the first days of class.

On the other hand, there are advantages to going alone to registration. If you can't get someone you know to go to college with you, get to know someone who wants to go to college or who is already enrolled in college. As you stand in those long lines or browse in the bookstore or wait in the student lounge between classes, talk to people. Sometimes it takes being able to make a first step toward friendship. Remember, other people are in the same boat you are in and may feel shy or out-of-place.

In addition to talking to people in various campus meeting places, talk to people in your classes. A few words passed before or after class can lead to a lasting friendship. And you need to get the phone number of at least one person in each of your classes so you can find out what happened in a class you missed for some reason. It works both ways; you can share information with others. But be careful about being used, and be careful whom you get information from. Some students will skip class repeatedly and expect to copy all your notes or let you do all the work on a group project. Choose your friends and study mates carefully. You don't need another child to raise.

Choosing professors or instructors

As I mentioned earlier, you can get information while standing in line at registration or in the student lounge. Students who have completed courses are more than willing to share their feelings about the course and the professor. However, this information isn't always reliable. For instance, a student may have a poor opinion of an instructor because of an incident that was actually the student's fault. As an example, I'll share this story.

Most schools have students evaluate teachers at the end of the semester. The teachers do not see the evaluations until well into the next semester, so students can be honest about the instructor and the course. At the university where I taught both as a graduate assistant and an adjunct professor, the students are given scantron sheets (for computer scoring) and questionnaires with a space to write a comment if they choose. The only negative comment I have ever received was, "The teacher spent too much time talking about current events and not enough about the assignments." Although the evaluation sheets are not signed, I believe I know who wrote the comment. He was a senior high school student who was concurrently enrolled in the second semester freshman composition course. He didn't have to take the first course because of his high SAT score. He was ranked in the top ten of his high school class, but his essays showed little thought and effort. He seemed to be satisfied with the grades on his papers (and unwilling to correct them) until the end of the semester when he asked what his final grade would be. When he discovered that he would make a B (and only because I give so much credit for class participation and activities was it that high), he started begging for an A: He needed an A for a scholarship. His dad was so-and-so, a very important person. His high school teachers let him do extra work to get an A, so why wouldn't I?

Well, I'm a reasonable person, and I certainly didn't want his grade in my class to cost him a scholarship (although I doubted that it would), but I could not give him an A. Other students in the class had put forth so much effort to receive A's, including another student from the same high school. Although not in the top ten percent of his class, he consistently turned in wonderful papers and had earned an A according to the grading system that I clearly outline in my syllabus. I could not in fairness give the B student an A. He was very upset when he discovered that I would not give in. When evaluation time came, he blamed me for the fact that he would receive a B. It was my fault, not his.

Although it bothered me that he was disappointed, I didn't take his comment as constructive criticism and revise my teaching strategies. Yes, we did talk about current events. We analyzed political speeches and advertising, a very important part of the course. But his claim that I didn't talk enough about the assignments, I knew was not true.

In addition to in-class instructions, I also have a typed hand-out for each assignment, outlining specifically what is expected. I also make sure the students have samples for each assignment and feel strongly that I'm right in doing so. (Another instructor told me that I shouldn't give students samples because they wouldn't have sample papers in the Real World. My response was that if students did write papers in the Real World, I would certainly encourage them to find examples before they start—as any professional writer would do.)

Now, I suspect this student would tell others to avoid taking my class. Yet, hundreds of others would enthusiastically recommend me. So, if possible, get a second opinion before you mark an instructor off your list. The following information will also help you choose professors, but keep in mind that you must know a little about an instructor's style to make an evaluation. So, rather than asking a former student whether an instructor is good or bad, ask some specific questions: Does the instructor respond well when a student asks a question, or does he or she seem irritated? Is the instructor available out of class for questions? Is he or she sexist or have some other obvious bias? Are the tests fair? Are assignments outlined? etc.

Kinds of instructors

Traditional freshmen pass the word about professors through fraternities and sororities and during lunchroom conversations and at night in the dormitory. As a non-resident, you will have to establish other contacts and ways of choosing professors. I mentioned earlier that you can collect information in the registration line, in the student lounge, etc., but you can also evaluate professors during the first days of class when you might still have the option of transferring to another class.

Teaching Assistants (TAs)

Freshman and sophomore courses are often taught by TAs at universities. TAs (called GAs or graduate assistants at some schools) are students themselves who may have just taken the minimum number of graduate courses required to teach or may be very close to earning doctorates. They may know a great deal about the subject area and know very little about the art of teaching. They may be on the young side and have big heads because they are college teachers and be more interested in the prestige or power than teaching. Some may feel threatened or intimidated by older students. They may worry that you will call them on something that you know more about than they do. And some might play to the younger students.

I once overheard an older man, after a first class meeting, say to a young TA (who was busily flirting with the pretty coeds) "Excuse me. I didn't get your name." The TA turned to the man and said glibly, "That's because I didn't give it." He then turned back to his flock of young students. I was hurt for the older man and embarrassed for the teaching profession. I believe that particular TA's attitude is a rare thing among TAs, and please don't get the idea that you should expect the same from a young TA. However, if you should encounter such an instructor, again, don't take it personally. Just get thee to the registrar and transfer to another class. You are paying for this experience. If you are attending a state-funded university or a community college, you are paying through taxes in addition to tuition. You have rights as a student and as a taxpayer—not to mention the respect you deserve as a human being.

I'm not saying that first impressions are always right. Instructors are not above having the same kind of first-day jitters that students have and may at first come across as aloof when actually they are not. And TAs and instructors of all levels sometimes find out at the last minute they will be teaching a class they didn't expected to teach and for which they are not yet prepared. After the first couple of classes, the teacher may seem to change entirely and the class may end up being a wonderful experience. And remember, you don't necessarily have to like an instructor's personality to learn from him or her.

I'm not advising you to avoid classes that are taught by TAs. Certainly, many young graduate assistants bring exuberance to the classroom that is sadly missing in the classrooms of some professors. A TA may be determined to do the best job ever at the university and may, in fact, carry out that goal. I have known TAs who had the time and energy to develop wonderful courses and cared enough to go an extra mile for each student. They, unlike some older professors, have not had time to "burn-out." Many are idealists who believe they are doing something worthwhile and who believe in students.

And not all TAs are young. Many are older students like yourself. In addition to teaching, they are enrolled in graduate courses. They may be enrolled in an internship program in which they teach one or two courses while taking from two to four courses. And many have families and even outside jobs. Getting a graduate degree may not require superior intelligence, but it certainly requires endurance. The following piece by Charlene Rodgers may help you understand what TAs face. When Charlene wrote this, she was teaching two classes as a TA, taking four graduate courses as a student, helping day and night to run a sheep farm, and keeping house and cooking for a husband and four children.

Considering Graduate School?

By Charlene Rodgers

Perhaps you just graduated from college with your B.A. or B.S. degree, or maybe you're thinking of returning for an advanced degree after being away from school for several years, and you're feeling afraid to start graduate school and/or applying for a graduate assistantship.

Well, you should be afraid.

If you value your marriage, family, health, or sanity, graduate school is not the place to be. Of course, if you are not married, don't have any children or friends, are chronically ill anyway, and look on a year or two in the state mental hospital as a rewarding holiday, go right ahead; graduate school and a graduate assistantship are just made for you. However, problems arise when you do have a spouse, children, friends, perfect check-ups, and prefer Miami Beach to Terrell or Wichita Falls [Texas cities with mental hospitals] but are lured on to enter graduate school anyway with promises of higher pay, better jobs, and ego-flattering prestige. Look again at what you're jumping into, what you really stand to gain, and who is painting that illusory picture.

In order to ascertain the precise effects of being a graduate student and having an assistantship, I made a not-too-random survey of twenty graduate students in the English department at East Texas State University; fifteen of these held graduate assistantships. Of those who were married, 85% said they thought they might be having "serious" marital problems; the remaining 15% had not seen their spouses in so long that they said it was hard to tell for sure. Of those having serious marital problems, 70% were either divorced or were going to see a lawyer as soon as they finished their term papers. Based on the data collected from those graduate students who had children, there seemed to be an inverse relationship between course teaching-taking load and quality of parenting; nevertheless, 90% of these student-parents, when pressed, could actually remember how many children they had. When questioned about friendships, 20% of the sample responded, "What's that?," 35% answered, "I recognize the word," 40% said, "Don't I wish," and 5% laughed.

Although the true effects of graduate school on health and sanity are difficult to evaluate before the graduate degree is completed, I did make an effort to gather information on at least the short-term effects. Of the twenty graduate students surveyed, 100% said they took one or more of the following drugs daily: gin-and-tonic, Tagamet, amitriptyline, black coffee, Atarax, mood elevators, and acetaminophen. In addition, 90% of the students reported needing daily maintenance doses of two or more of these, while 55% stated that they also felt the need to cry, meditate, and/or scream at least four to seven times a week. Of the graduate students holding assistantships, 16% had already had stomach surgery, 33% were currently under the care of psychiatrists, and 8% were unavailable to respond due to hospitalization.

If you are still considering graduate school and statistics don't impress you, look at all the benefits you may reap from your hard-won degree once they let you out of the state hospital. First, you'll be free and unencumbered by a spouse, children, or friends, which will make it easy for you to take a job almost anywhere—like Passos, Brazil or Tajarhi, Libya. And that's a good thing if you want to teach in college; with the job market so tight and with your medical history, those are probably the only places that might hire you. Of course, if you are interested in high school teaching, you won't have any trouble getting a job, and with the automatic pay increase, after the doctor and lawyer are paid off you will probably realize only a small net loss overall. Also, if you're careful not to mention your doctorate or master's degree, most of the other teachers will soon forget. Actually it's best not to mention your degree at all since the only person that's likely to be impressed is someone else crazy enough to go to graduate school himself—which brings me to the person who might try to lure you into entering graduate school in the first place . . . on second thought . . . no . . . just let me finish this basket, and I'll show you around the department.

Charlene's essay reflects some of the frustration felt not only by adult TAs but also by adult students in general. However, the up side is Charlene now has a senior editor position at one of the country's leading publishers. So don't be discouraged; just remember that TAs are human, too, and they have many of the same difficulties, obstacles, and frustrations that you do.

Community college instructors

Some two-year colleges hire instructors who have master's degrees in their fields, rather than doctorates. I have heard that some colleges prefer master-degreed instructors because they can pay them less. Certainly, if there is truth in that rumor, it would depend on the policy of the individual school. But most colleges do want instructors with doctorates and try to search out the best in the field, even though they are competing with the more prestigious universities. The work load is usually greater in community colleges, but the pay may not be.

Many colleges do, however, hire a healthy percentage of adjunct, or part-time instructors, instead of adding full-time positions. This is partly because of fluctuating enrollment and partly because they can pay the adjuncts peanuts. Some schools have worked hordes of adjuncts for years, always holding the full-time-position carrot in front of them. So, it makes sense that sooner or later some of these adjuncts will get discouraged, disgruntled—peeved. If an instructor begins the first class with a report on the "lousy school," you may be better off to transfer to another class; that instructor may not be motivated to put forth his or her best effort.

Some community colleges also hire adjuncts who teach full-time in high schools. These folks are real troopers. Spending all day at a high school, not to mention actually *teaching* 100-plus students (some of whom want to shoot off her or his kneecaps), is physically and mentally exhausting. Those who have anything left to give to night college classes *can* be excellent instructors. However, few teachers can give

100 percent in the public-school classroom and still have 100 percent to give to an evening class.

As for the full-timers, whether a teacher has a master's degree or a doctorate doesn't determine the kind of teacher he or she is, especially for lower-level (freshman and sophomore) classes. Very often, community colleges seek instructors who are very student-oriented, who care about the needs of students and are willing to spend time helping individual students. And instructors at community colleges are usually not under the pressure to "publish or perish" and have more time available for students.

University professors

At the university level, teachers (other than TAs) are either instructors, assistant professors, associate professors, professors, or if they are part-time, adjunct instructors or professors. Their rank depends on their time and achievements in their fields. University teachers are under pressure to publish in the journals in their fields, to write books, to give presentations at conferences, to serve on committees, and to participate in a number of other activities that prove that they know what they are talking about. They are sometimes preoccupied with making names for themselves in their fields. They are sometimes so knowledgeable in and dedicated to their fields that they are accused of living in "ivory towers" far above the masses. Some of them became college professors because of their love of the subject areas and desire to do research, not because of their love of teaching. Others love both their subject areas and teaching others, sharing their knowledge.

Good teachers have certain characteristics. First of all, they know their subject areas. Notice that I said *know their subject areas* instead of *knew their subject areas*. Knowledge changes, and good teachers are constantly up-dating their knowledge. If a teacher is still lecturing from the yellowed notes that he or she took twenty or thirty years ago when in college, chances are that teacher is not a good one. You will probably hear jokes about professors who have been dead for years and still walk the halls. (We're not talking about ghosts here).

But being up-to-date is not the only thing that makes a teacher a good teacher. A good teacher uses whatever creative and imaginative devices necessary to get information across to students. A good teacher is interested in helping students learn how to learn, rather than just making sure students memorize lists of facts. You can learn from someone who knows the content area but is short on teaching skills. You simply have to put forth more effort yourself. Some teachers make learning interesting; others do not. I recently heard someone say that good teachers don't really teach; they present the information in such a way that students can't resist learning. I often think of M.I.T.'s John Hildebidle's statement about teaching. He said, "I would wish to be remembered less for what I knew or said than for what others figured out, in my presence, how to do. An effective teacher is one who, to an unusual degree, seems just to happen to be nearby when dawn comes." Good teachers help students make their own discoveries.

But what if you walk into a class and find that the instructor makes obvious attempts to scare the hell out of everybody with statements such as "Only half of you will pass this course"? Well, some teachers use scare tactics to cut down the class size. Certainly, if half the class drops, the other half will pass if they do the work. Instructors who employ such scare tactics may be trying to run off students who are not willing to put forth a real effort. They may also be trying to cut down on their paper loads. If an instructor has several classes, grading papers can be tedious and time-consuming.

And I know of a professor who "flunked" an entire class because she was assigned to teach a class she didn't want to teach.

But professors like the above mentioned are rare—well, maybe not rare. Some students claim the percentage of good to bad teachers is about 60/40. Yes, there are many professors who are real jerks—self-absorbed elitists who have tenure (a permanent job, no matter how well they perform). But these folks are fairly easy to spot on the first day of class when there is still time to drop and add (change classes). If you do end up with a professor who has unrealistic expectations, seems to use scare tactics to weed out students, or fails to really teach the material, make appointments with him or her for clarification on class lectures, material covered on tests, etc. Often a student who shows a determination to dig will find a teacher willing to help him or her learn.

Students have told me about professors who have come to school drunk and fallen over while lecturing (one guy briefly continued the lecture from his place on the floor and then curtly dismissed the class). One woman told me about a professor who scratched his crotch while lecturing. She said she was distracted, wondering what kind of vermin he had and, more importantly, how far they could jump. She moved from the front to the back row.

Yet most professors are not only top-notch teachers but also top-notch human beings and interested in promoting knowledge as a way of advancing the cause of humanity. These professors are available to students who really want to learn. It may take some effort to make sure your classes are taught by the best professors, but it's worth it.

Survival Tip

Read the books or articles your professors have published. In addition to learning content, you will learn something about the authors.

Students have told me about outstanding instructors— creative teachers who made the subject matter interesting and warm teachers who made students feel special. If possible, I pass on the compliments to the teacher. As a student, I had professors who had shortcomings but from whom I learned a great deal. I had a few really exceptional professors; I could count them on one hand. But I never dropped a course because of a professor, perhaps because I had such low expectations from my public school days. I recently called to thank the two public school teachers I remembered as outstanding—second- and ninth-grade teachers. Both had retired; one was 85 years old. Each was thrilled to be remembered and to know that she had influenced me. Teachers' rewards may come twenty or thirty years after the fact, but outstanding teachers live on in the hearts of all their students. (Does this make you want to be one of those teachers or, perhaps, track down the good teachers in your life and thank them?)

Buying textbooks

You may have a severe case of sticker shock when you visit the college bookstore. Textbooks prices have increased dramatically in recent years, perhaps because publishers have to make their money off the first sales of a new edition. After the first sales, used book vendors and bookstores make the money. Students sell their textbooks back to the bookstore for, say, $12, and the bookstore sells the same book the next semester for $30 or so, a few dollars less than the price of a new book. You get the picture. That's why publishers release new editions of textbooks every few years. But your problem is how to get the books you need without breaking your budget.

You can sometimes get by with using an old edition (especially literature books) that you can buy at an off-campus used bookstore. Instructors tend to stay with the selections they know, the selections that were in the old edition. The page numbers may be different, but chances are the old edition will have everything you need.

The college bookstore will have courses listed and the textbooks that are used for those courses. Sometimes book lists are made up by committees for lower level classes, and sometimes those committees have several books listed for one course, books that every instructor may not use. So wait until after the first class to buy books. The instructor may tell you the book won't be used or may have it on reserve in the library. You may be able to borrow the book from the library or from another student who used it the previous semester.

Ludy Gibson said she managed to get good deals on textbooks by looking around the cafeteria or other places for students who were carrying books she would need the next semester. She would ask them if they planned to sell their books back and, if so, arrange to buy it at the end of the semester for the same price the bookstore was paying.

The first class

First classes, whether kindergarten or graduate level, share this: the students have a high anxiety level. The anxiety is partly from excitement and partly from fear. After months of kindergarten, my niece told her mother that she had finally "stopped being afraid." I have taught ninth-grade boys who tried to be their idea of macho on first class days but who wrote later in their journals that they had been terrified. First class days of new stages—elementary school, junior high, high school, college—are frightening. And for adult students who have been out of school for years and who feel out of touch with institutionalized education, the fear is compounded. Brad Price was just out of the Marine Corps when he enrolled in college. Toward the end of his first semester, he wrote this in his journal:

> The classroom was cold and quiet at first. I picked out a seat in the back. School—the thought of it made my hands shake and stomach turn. The walls were yellow and dull. There weren't any desks—just three rows of tables with about five tables to a row. No one said a word, and— damn, I thought I was going to freeze.
>
> The teacher walked in. She looked like my third-grade teacher Mrs. Peerbody. Great! What a wonderful way to start a new life. I didn't know anyone. It was cold, and the same teacher who told me I was going to grow up and live on skid row was here.
>
> However, I eventually met everyone; the classroom became warmer; and the teacher wasn't my third-grade teacher. (I found out later that Mrs. Peerbody died in a motorcycle accident when her Harley slammed into an El Dorado.) With the way everything turned out, my English class became one of my favorites.

Well, there can only be one first class day per semester; it will pass. Try to concentrate on listening well, scooping out the territory, and smiling at others who may be desperately in need of empathy. You will find that meeting and talking to other people will ease the tension and fear. You may meet someone who not only shares your feelings but also is a good candidate for car-pooling with you.

Chapter 5
College Protocol: The Spoken and Unspoken Rules

How to be a good student

Good students have certain things in common. They are prepared for what they will do in class. They have textbooks with them, have read the assignment, and are prepared to discuss it, asking questions about anything they did not understand. They have pen and paper ready to take notes or do in-class activities. They attend all classes and sit as close as possible to the instructor, listening attentively. They take notes, jotting down key concepts and terms to review later (see Chapter 6). They make sure they understand all assignments and complete them on time.

As you go through college, you will probably hear things about certain instructors (ie., "To make an A in his class, laugh at his jokes" or "You have to kiss ass in her class to make a good grade"). Students sometimes believe that having something in common with the instructor will make a difference. I taught a second-semester freshman composition class in which almost half the students had been in my composition class the previous semester. These students had picked up on the fact that I like Mark Twain, probably because of the number of times had I quoted him or used examples from his work to make a point about writing. I asked the students to interview and then introduce each other to the class, telling why the partner deserved space on this planet (what they had done or planned to do).

The introductions started, and the first couple of students introduced had told their partners that Mark Twain was their favorite author. (They had not been asked to give a favorite author.) The class caught on (I cracked up laughing), and by the time the introductions were finished, everyone's favorite author was Mark Twain.

Although this incident started (and proceeded) as a joke, some students do try to find out things about instructors so that they can "share" those things, hoping it will improve their grades. As a general rule, though, hard work gets the rewards. Experienced teachers have been conned, brown-nosed, buttered-up, and so forth enough to recognize the attempt, and usually they are immune. But let me add this: Teachers of all levels are human. I have known some who had tremendous egos and who liked to have those egos fed. I have known some who had fairly limited knowledge even about what they were teaching and who, consequently, hated for students to ask questions because they might not be able to answer them. Obviously, no teacher can know *everything*. Most are willing to admit it when they do not have an answer to a question. They often research the question and provide an answer at a later time. Sometimes, if the question is relevant to the entire class, the instructor may ask students to contribute their ideas.

The bottom line is that there are as many different kinds of teachers as there are different personalities in general. The knowledge about human nature that you have gained through experience in dealing with friends, relatives, neighbors, employers, etc. will help you "read" teachers and respond to them appropriately.

Survival Tip

Never ask an instructor whether you will do anything "important" in class on a given day. (This is a common question from students who need or want to be absent from class or leave early.)

Classroom behavior

Teachers have preferences about the way students conduct themselves in class, about classroom atmosphere in general, and about how assignments should be done. First, let's talk about how students conduct themselves. As a general rule, don't talk to the person sitting next to you when the instructor (or another classmate) is talking. I'm sure this makes perfect sense to you. No speaker likes to be distracted by audience chatter, but the main thing is that noise in the audience is distracting to other students who are trying to hear what the speaker is saying. In the first couple of classes in a Composition II course, I noticed that two young women in the back of the room were constantly whispering to each other, especially when I talked about assignments. After class I mentioned to one of them that it would be hard for them to hear and understand me if they were conversing with each other. The young woman told me that the student next to her kept asking her what I had just said.

Okay, the conversation was about the course, as is usually the case with chatter in a college class. The two were not talking about their boyfriends, or whatever. But the second student was deprived of hearing what she needed to know because the first student had poor listening skills and was depending on the person sitting next to her to explain everything instead of listening carefully to what I was saying.

The first student might have solved her problem by sitting near the front or recording the class and replaying it at another time.

While it is true that sometimes the mind wanders and we miss something a speaker is saying, the time to get clarification is after class or with a question to the instructor. If you think you may have missed something important, jot down some key words to remind yourself what the information referred to, and ask the instructor (at an appropriate time) to repeat that part of the material. And if you heard the information but are not sure exactly what it meant, ask the instructor to clarify. Yes, some instructors get impatient with questions about what was just said. In some large lecture classes, questions will not be encouraged at all. But most instructors are happy to repeat the material, and a question from you indicates that others might be having the same problems with understanding the information. So, avoid the temptation to ask the person sitting next to you what was just said, especially while the instructor is still talking. And move away from someone who talks to you at inappropriate times.

You will probably find it best to sit near the front. Often students who are not really serious about learning sit in the back of the room, and their behavior can be distracting. If you sit on the front row, take notes, and show an interest in what the instructor is saying, you will probably gain the instructor's favor early on. Any speaker likes to see signs he or she is being heard. Occasionally nodding in agreement, showing interest through facial expressions, and taking notes at appropriate times will tell the instructor you are paying attention.

Reading, cleaning out your purse or notebook, and chewing gum are also distracting to an instructor. Although you can listen and make paper airplanes at the same time, such activities suggest you are not listening and are not taking the speaker seriously. I heard a story about a student who was reading a newspaper as he sat front-row, center during a lecture. The instructor snatched up the newspaper, flung it in the wastebasket, and asked the student to leave the class.

Instructors complain about students who don't have manners enough to remove their hats or caps in the classroom. While hats on the back row probably won't bother anyone (except, perhaps, the instructor), hats on other rows can be distracting and block other students' view of the instructor or of the board and other visual aids. (Think of trying to see around a fat head of hair in a movie theater; some hats are worse.)

Here are some general rules for classroom behavior:

1. Sit up straight, pen and paper at hand, and listen attentively to the instructor.
2. Save your questions until after the instructor has finished his sentence. (Don't blurt out a question or comment while the instructor is still talking.)
3. Indicate that you would like to have the floor by raising your hand or otherwise indicating to the instructor that you have something to say.
4. Have any questions or comments jotted down on paper so you won't have to ramble on until you think of what you wanted to say.
5. Make sure you clearly understand instructions about assignments. If you don't understand everything the instructor said, make notes about questions you want to ask or things you want to look up in the text later. If you seem to be less prepared than the others in the class, you might have to do a lot of digging when you get home or even get a personal tutor.
6. Save your conversation with the person sitting next to you until after class.

7. Don't smack gum, eat crackers, click your pen, kick the chair in front of you, or move your chair repeatedly.

8. Don't go to class half-dressed from your aerobics class or wear caps or hats in class.

Survival Tip

Ask a question during the last five minutes of class at your own risk. Students who ask a lot of questions irritate other students, particularly when dismissal of class is delayed.

Also, don't block the aisle when class is dismissed if you value your body. Some students have only ten minutes between classes—ten minutes to cross the campus, go over notes for a test, smoke a cigarette, make a phone call, or try to catch a glimpse of a girl- or boyfriend. While some instructors (unthoughtfully) will hold classes beyond the scheduled time, it is irritating, maddening, to some students to be held over. Many students who don't have back-to-back classes are still ready to clear the room when class is over. With younger students, the hurry to leave class may be a carry-over from their high school days when they had only five minutes to go to their lockers and join the stampede to the next class. From my student days, I remember feeling resentment and anxiety while being held over by an instructor. If I didn't have another class, I had 70 miles to drive or library work to do. On the other hand, I have had students who stayed after class, talking to me for as long as 30 minutes. And that's fine, but, I repeat, don't block the aisle.

Another thing that irritates instructors and other students alike are personal, boring, unrelated monologues that go something like this: "You know my cousin—well, she wasn't really my cousin. She was married to my—well, he worked at the Ford plant before he was fired for releasing a greased pig in the executive offices. But anyway, my cousin—well, she had that same experience back in 1972—no, it must have been 1973, well, maybe it was 1974. Oh, well. But really . . . ."

Talk about kids or grandkids, no matter how exceptional they are, usually falls in the same category. As you might guess, adult students, especially those who have not been in the workforce for years and who have had mostly preschoolers and pets to talk to, are tempted to catch up on social discourse. But it doesn't win popularity. Make sure what you say in class is relevant and brief.

You may find, however, that you and other adult students do most of the responding to the instructor's questions. Younger students are often more concerned about what their peers think of them than are adult students, especially during the first few classes. As I mentioned earlier, younger students might actually depend on you to answer. A long silence after a question has been thrown out by the instructor makes students nervous; the instructor just might start singling out students to answer.

You may even start to feel like the lone voice and wonder what other students are thinking. Lisa, an adult student who often speaks out in class, said, "The reality is you usually don't know what others really think of you. My experience in class is that very few students comment on my behavior until much later on in the semester. Then I end up with my own cheering section, enemies, or—well, you never know what some people think."

However, even though you will probably know the answer to most of the instructors questions because you read the assignment and reflected on it, refrain from raising your hand to answer every time to give younger students a chance to answer. One adult student told me she almost has to sit on her hands to keep from raising them. She knows the answers or has a comment to make each time I ask for a response, but she realizes other students also have something to say. She also realizes that I need to hear from other students. I already know she is thinking.

What do you call the instructor?

Most instructors will write a name on the board or syllabus, clearly indicating whether they are to be called Dr., Professor, Mr., Mrs., or Ms. So-and-so. Some instructors will tell the class what he or she prefers to be called; others will leave it up to the students. Young students feel more comfortable using titles. They have just finished 12 years of school in which every teacher was a title (Mr., Mrs., Coach, etc.) and a last name. They will be expected to use that form for other instructors.

In community college classes with a mix of older and younger students, I tell them to call me what they feel comfortable calling me, either by my first name or title and last name. I want the classroom atmosphere to be relaxed. I also want students to feel comfortable, and I usually already know some of the students. I have found that older students usually call me by my first name and younger students usually call me Dr. Schindley. I do not want to imply, however, that all professors feel the same or even that my position is correct. Most instructors prefer a more formal atmosphere and consider it an affront, or simply bad manners, when a student uses a first name address. So this is something you will have to pick up from individual instructors. To be on the safe side, if you are not told otherwise, use the title and last name.

I still use the Dr. title when I address some of my former professors. I recently received an e-mail from one of my former professors who said, "I thought I told you years ago to stop calling me Dr. My name is Richard." He did, but old habits die hard, and, well, he's still my teacher.

Pretty papers

Although most teachers do not consciously grade a paper on how it looks, teachers are human. Reading an almost illegible paper is trying on the eyes and on the patience. When you turn in assignments, make sure that they are neatly written on standard notebook paper (unless otherwise specified). Almost all instructors will recoil from a paper that is written on paper that has been torn from a spiral notebook. The edges cause the pages to stick together and, well, they make a stack of to-be-graded papers look higher and messier. How the paper looks has nothing to do with the content, but still, you are dealing with humans. Even a subconscious aversion to how a paper looks might affect the grade. Again, I will say that most instructors would not consciously grade a paper on how it looks, unless, of course, you are given specific instructions and choose to ignore them.

Essays and research papers should be typed if possible. Some instructors will require that you type all papers; others will not. But typed papers are much easier to read. If you don't know how to type, consider taking a typing course during your first semester or using a computer program to learn typing. If you have a computer at home, you might try one of the programs that type as you speak, but don't choose the night before a paper is due to learn to use the program. If you don't have a computer at home, most campuses have them available for students in either the library, a computer lab, or in a writing skills center.

When comparing typewriters to word processing, the computer wins every time. Earlier I mentioned a woman who stayed up half the night typing a perfect copy of her paper.

With a word processor, the task would have taken only a few minutes. If you don't have computer experience, don't let that keep you from taking advantage of this wonderful technology. Word processing programs are "user friendly": you don't need experience to use them because the programs themselves teach you how to operate them. With a couple of questions to a lab assistant in the computer center or writing lab, you can produce a paper, print it out, revise it at home, and correct it back at the lab before you print out a final, correct copy.

Actually, you should always print out *two* copies or make a photocopy. Never turn in the only copy of a paper. Accidents happen. Student papers have been lost—have disappeared. A respected and responsible professor at a large university took a stack of 20-page term papers to a coffee shop to grade. He left the table for a minute, and the papers disappeared. But the possibility it may be lost by an instructor is not the only reason to keep a copy of your paper. You may need to discuss material contained in the paper in class, or you may need some of the information for a test or another class before the instructor grades and returns the paper.

Finding out early what your instructor expects is important. Some instructors will allow neat, hand-written corrections on final drafts; others frown on anything but a clean paper. If you are using a typewriter, one way to make small corrections is to use white-out (correction fluid) on the mistake, type over the error, and make a copy of the corrected page. The correction will not show on the copy. Of course, computers make all that trouble unnecessary, but you may still have last-minute corrections.

Papers should be typed in manuscript form unless you are given specific instructions otherwise. Research papers for most classes can be documented using MLA (Modern Language Association) style, unless you are given other instructions. You will probably be asked to use APA

(American Psychological Association) style for documentation of papers in psychology and ASA (American Sociological Association) style for papers in sociology classes. In science classes, you may be asked to use another style. (See Chapter 9 for manuscript and documentation style.)

In summary, the written assignments and papers you turn in should be neat and relatively error free. We'll talk about content and correctness in other chapters, but here I refer mainly to the appearance of a paper. Scribbled cross-outs, ragged paper, and sloppy handwriting send the message that the writer simply doesn't care much about the work. If you must make a correction on a paper that you will not be able to recopy, make a single straight line through the material you want to delete. Again, take notebook paper to class for in-class assignments so you will not have to tear paper from your spiral notebook. And practice your handwriting skills if you have a habit of making ill-formed letters. People who have not practiced writing much devote much mental energy to forming characters—mental energy that is needed to express ideas. With practice you will train yourself to write neatly without thinking about it, so your real concentration can be on *what* you are writing instead of *how* you are writing it. If you have a habit of printing instead of writing, it will probably be to your advantage to practice cursive writing. To some instructors, printing looks elementary. It will take some practice to change this habit, but it may pay off.

Remember also to read over everything you write before you turn it in. You can catch and neatly correct your own errors for free. If the instructor corrects your errors or wonders what in the world you are trying to say, it will cost you.

The language of the classroom

In the old days, we talked about Standard English as correct English. The textbooks had examples of Standard English and Non-Standard English; the Standard English example was right, and the Non-Standard example was wrong. Today we talk about Edited American English and regional and cultural dialects. The purpose of language is to communicate messages, and people all over America communicate just fine in dialects that are not what you hear on the six o'clock news. So, the different regional and cultural dialects are not wrong. They are simply the language that is used in certain situations—with family and friends. What we try to do now is give speakers of various dialects a tool they can use in the classroom and in the work world. We know that having the ability to speak and write Edited American English can help people move up the socioeconomic ladder. However, we also admit that a slip of the tongue or an error in writing will not condemn anyone to the firing squad. The men and women who speak on the networks are trained to speak a certain dialect—a dialect that typifies what is correct and proper in this country. Yet even the well-trained announcers sometimes make errors. Wolf Blitzer, CNN's Washington correspondent and very articulate speaker of Edited American English, during the Gulf War responded to an anchorperson's question with "Alls I know . . ." If you listen closely, you will hear newspeople, statespeople, and actors use *probly* instead of *probably*. But these people are not discredited because of a mere slip of tongue. In fact, if we used the approach of *describing* rather than *proscribing* the language of Americans, the word *probly* would be more correct than *probably*. The language is constantly changing—even Edited American English.

So, let's examine the term *Edited American English*. The word *edited* implies that it has been corrected—that the speech has been learned and practiced or that writing has been checked for deviations. *American* differentiates it from British English, a different dialect. Edited American English is the language of the American culture—the language of the media and the business world. The hillbilly sentence "I ain't got no time for that" and the black dialect sentence "I reads novels" both communicate ideas effectively. But we know the language is not the language we hear or read in the media or in the business and academic worlds.

Edited American English is the language of the culture as a whole, but there are thousands of subcultures within the larger culture. Each of these subcultures has its own language, whether the subculture is based on location, on race, or on age. Teenagers, for instance, have a certain language to use when communicating with each other, but they are not likely to use that language when communicating with the high school principal or even with their parents. One reason for this is they might not be understood. Adults must be taught the new slang words of teens. Another reason is that teen slang is a kind of secret code that they tend to protect from adults who might borrow (and massacre) teen language.

Most of us have several languages. We have the language we use when speaking to a baby; we have the language we use when speaking to our friends; we have the language we use when speaking to our employers. What we try to do in English class is make sure students have the tool of Edited American English to use when the situation calls for it. They might not use it at home, and they might not use it when speaking to friends, but they will be able to function in the business and academic worlds without feeling handicapped by their speech differences. In other words, Edited American English is a tool to keep in your back pocket and use when you need it. One of the times you need it is when writing papers for classes in college, but that certainly is not the only time you need it.

So, learning Edited American English for use in the classroom and the business world makes sense because it works in those situations (see Chapter 8). We keep our regional or racial or age group dialects for use when they work best.

Presentations

In some classes, you will be asked to make presentations, or speeches, to the class. Your first response might be panic, especially if you have not had much practice speaking before audiences. My advice here is to remember that others are feeling discomfort, too. You are not the only one in the whole world who is nervous when speaking to an audience. Remember also that no one (to my knowledge) has ever died from stage fright. You may think it is obvious to everyone that your knees are shaking, that your heart is pounding, that you are perspiring, that your voice sounds unnatural, but it is not. Often the others in the class are worrying so much about what they will do when their turn comes that they would hardly notice if your skirt fell off.

Here are some tips:

1. Prepare for the day by getting in a relaxed state and imagining giving the speech calmly and enjoying the experience. In other words, instead of thinking about the speech and allowing yourself to feel panic, teach yourself to associate giving a speech with a feeling of relaxation. Don't allow yourself to build up negativity by dwelling on all the horrible things that could possibly happen. Yes, you could faint. Yes, everyone in the audience could sit there

and glare at you. But those things will not happen. Giving a speech is a wonderful opportunity to share with others. It is also practice that will help you become a better speaker.

2. Know your subject. Be well prepared. If you are given a choice for your topic, choose something that you already know about and, preferably, something that not many others know about. You want to be the most informed person in the room about your subject. If you already know something about the subject, you are less likely to forget the material, lose your train of thought, and finding yourself standing awkwardly mute in front of the class. If you are not given complete freedom in choosing a topic, you might be able to slant the speech toward something you know about or relate it to knowledge you already have. I once had to give a presentation on textual analysis, which has to do with discovering the origin of errors in books. The errors may be caused by the author himself, by translators, by editors, by type-setters, or by machines that set the type for printing.

I had worked on a newspaper, so I incorporated a story about a reporter who was writing about the activities of a visiting celebrity. Instead of writing "He made a raid on the magazine rack at the hotel news stand," the reporter wrote "He laid a maid on the magazine rack at the hotel news stand." I wrote the sentences on the board and discussed the implications of misspelling or transposing words during the writing process, and I talked about what happens during the typesetting and proofreading processes at newspapers. The story was a hit, but I certainly didn't feel like an expert in textual analysis.

3. Take a few deep breaths before you begin, and tell yourself that speaking will be a pleasant experience because you *want* to share the information you have with others.

4. Dress comfortably in something that makes you feel good and that won't show perspiration stains if you don't trust your deodorant. The last thing you need is to wonder whether you should keep your arms pinned to your sides to hide wet circles. Glance in a mirror before class so you will be satisfied that you look nice and that you don't have spinach on your teeth.

5. Use visual aids or hand-outs to focus attention away from yourself as a speaker and toward the information itself. Doing something with your hands will make you feel less self-conscious. You might write on the board or write material on a transparency to show the audience with a projector.

6. You could try the Dale Carnigie approach: Picture the audience as sitting there in their underwear. People are fairly non-threatening in their underwear.

7. If you have a choice, volunteer to be first. You can then sit back and enjoy the other presentations with a friendly smile or interested look on your face for the benefit of the other speakers. You also have the advantage of not being compared to anyone else as you give your presentation. Going last often means having some hard acts to follow.

8. Pick two or three people at random spots around the room and keep your eyes moving from one to the others. This will help you overcome the temptation to focus on one person who seems to be listening and responding in a positive way.

Chapter 6
How to Study

One of the common concerns of adult students or adults considering college is wondering whether they have forgotten how to study. A more accurate description might be that they were never taught to study effectively. I say this because of my own experience; I don't remember getting any instruction in the art of studying in high school or college either. And I don't think things have changed much because a large percentage of young students don't really know how to study efficiently. They may study, and they may study often, but the art of studying productively is not something they can forget if they haven't learned it.

Learning styles or *brain power*

To learn the art of studying, first analyze yourself, your personal learning habits, then develop a strategy for studying, a systematic method that works best for *you*. What follows may be more than you want to know about the brain, but if you will take the quiz in this section and use your analysis of your habits and the tips, you can develop the art of studying. The results will be better grades and less time spent on learning the material you need to learn for classes.

First, most of us know very little about the approximately three-pound mass of nerve cells and their connectors that make up the brain. We leave that area to the scientists. But some knowledge of the brain is important to knowledge of personal learning styles. The following is Dr. Diane Hudson's explanation of brain functioning as related to learning. After Diane taught this material to her twelfth-grade honors class, one of the students became very angry. He demanded to know why he was just then, as a senior, learning this material. He said he should have been introduced to this material in elementary school. He was right, of course, and this material is being worked into the curriculum in some states. The National Association of Secondary School Principals has been a leader in supporting research in "brain-based education." The May, 1998, issue of *Bulletin*, the association's journal, contains nine articles on brain-based education. However, early on, scientists were concerned about misuse of information and, especially, the terms *left-brain* and *right-brain*. Much of the early information left the impression that we use exclusively one side of the brain or the other for tasks when, in fact, there is constant interplay between the hemispheres of the brain. Other critics say the idea that everyone is the same regarding which side of the brain is responsible for various tasks is wrong—that some people might have "left-brain" functions in the right side (see more on criticism and research below).

When something as complicated as brain research is translated into lay terms, certain facts and concepts tend to be misunderstood. So, keep in mind that the terms *left-brain* and *right-brain* are no longer politically correct; the terms *analytical* and *global* are now used by some researchers. However, much can be learned from brain research when applied to developing study skills. So here is Diane's lecture. You don't have to understand all the information to relate it to your own experience.

Learning Styles[*]
(Teaching notes from Dr. Diane Hudson)

The cells of the brain form separate structures. The largest and most sophisticated structure in the brain is the cerebral cortex, which is divided into a right and left hemisphere. The brain has an electrical system which, when stimulated, sends a message through pathways to centers in the brain. The brain also has a chemical system which blocks or allows transmission of the message. An interesting fact about this transmission process concerns memory. When you memorize something, the chemical system actually alters your brain physically. The chemicals leave a "track," like a scar or a permanent film, a physical record of the memory. It may be that each time you repeat, rewrite, or rehear something, the track is made stronger. Researchers have found that there are tricks—strategies—that help "lay the track" more solidly. These strategies consist of getting the brain's attention. Examples are highlighting important items with color or associating a word or idea with a picture. As we learn more about how our brains work, we can better learn to manipulate and control our brains and thus get more and better work out of them with less trouble to ourselves.

Much of our understanding of brain function—the jobs the brain can do and which part of the brain does those jobs—has come from the study of victims of brain injury or disease, such as epilepsy. Epilepsy is the name given to recurring seizures, or convulsions, of nerves in the left and right sides of the brain, or cerebral hemispheres. During the 1960's one of the treatments for severe epilepsy was cutting the major nerve pathway connecting the two sides of the brain. Because the left and right "brains" are normally in constant interaction with each other, when a

---

[*] This material was previously published in *The English Teacher's Guide to the Essential Elements*, Schindley and Hudson, DPC, 1985.

seizure began in one hemisphere, it almost always spreads to the other side. Cutting the connector, the corpus callosum, reduced the frequency and severity of the patients' seizures because a seizure in one hemisphere could no longer be transmitted to the other side. The advantage of this treatment was that the patients no longer suffered from such severe epilepsy. The disadvantage was that their left brains literally did not know what their right brains were doing, and the left and right brains must interact with each other constantly for the total brain to function properly.

Brain researchers, led by Roger Sperry, spent many years testing these "split-brain" patients. The descriptions of the tests are interesting in themselves. An example described in *The Social Brain* (Gazzaniga 198)[*] shows how closely the two sides of the brain must work together to produce thoughts and actions normal-brain people take for granted. Using high-tech projectors, the researchers flashed pictures on a screen in such a way and with such speed that only the left eye (controlled by the right brain) could see the image. When the patient was asked to point to a picture he had seen before, he could do so with his left hand (right brain). When he was asked what he had seen, he said, "Nothing." When asked why he had moved his left hand, he said he didn't know or suggested a reason which did not include the real motivation—seeing the picture. The right brain controls the left eye and hand and is very good at seeing patterns and matching pictures, but in the split-brain patient, the right brain was unable to communicate its information—"I just saw the same picture of a man on a bicycle."—to the left brain, and it could not verbalize, it could not speak, the information directly by itself. It could understand the words spoken to it, but it couldn't speak

---

[*] Michael Gazzaniga, *The Social Brain: Discovering the Networks of the Mind.* New York: Basic, 1985.

words. The left brain did not know why the right brain had moved the left hand.

Researchers used many precise tests to discover which part of the brain controls each specific task the brain/body must do for us to function normally. In tests like the one described above, time after time, the results showed that the right brain is chiefly nonverbal, that it cannot talk. It must convey its information to the left brain for that information to be turned into speech. At the same time, researchers found that the speech of split-brain patients was strangely unemotional. Verbal responses are often spoken with no expression of emotion at all. The voices, the speaking personalities, are flat, giving the listener no clues concerning the attitude of the speaker. The left brain controls speaking; the right brain controls both the perception and expression of emotion. If your left brain were disconnected from your right brain, you might sound like a robot when you said, "I love you" to someone. (You would, however, be able to put your left arm around him/her because the right, emotional brain also controls movement of the left arm.)

Many tests with the same results have given brain researchers some confidence that they understand—in a very small way—which parts of the brain do which jobs. There are still different theories concerning exactly how the brain is structured and where many functions occur in the brain. Researchers do know that our left and right brains have different jobs, skills, talents. The information is very important to us as learners because in most adults one hemisphere is dominant, especially when it comes to important but everyday life skills like problem solving and learning. That is, adults and many teenagers depend mainly on the skills of one "brain" to do such varied activities as taking notes in class, studying for a major exam, decorating a house, deciding to marry someone. All researchers insist emphatically that neither side of the brain is able to work without the other side. Split-brain patients are severely disabled in many ways. That is probably one reason doctors no longer treat epilepsy by cutting the corpus callosum. And all are adamant in their belief that we use very little of the potential power of our brains and that the first step is learning to use both sides equally well.

The following quiz may give you some insight into your own learning preferences.

Learning Styles Quiz

Circle or write the letter of the answer that best describes your usual behavior or attitude. There are no wrong answers. Answer quickly. Your first response is usually the "correct" one. If you cannot decide whether a. or b. applies most to you, put a star by the number.

1. Do you memorize/remember information best when you
   a. hear it
   b. see it

2. If you were trying to put something together (bicycle, toy, model airplane), which would you do first?
   a. read the instructions
   b. hold the parts and examine them to see how they fit

3. Which would you rather read or look at for information?
   a. a paragraph
   b. a drawing/diagram/graph

4. Which do you prefer to read?
   a. nonfiction (factual information)
   b. fiction (stories, plays, novels)

5. Which do you spend more time doing?
   a. planning
   b. dreaming

6. Which classroom situation do you prefer, assuming that the workload and difficulty are the same?
   a. a quiet, orderly class in which everything goes according to an announced schedule
   b. a sometimes noisy class in which students move around the room and work independently

7. When you read a story, you
   a. read for facts and details—the information.
   b. read for the sights, sounds, emotions, the picture and feeling of the story.

8. To find your way to a new place, you prefer
   a. specific verbal directions (Go two blocks; turn right.)
   b. a map of the area.

9. Which side of the classroom do you prefer?
   a. left side
   b. right side

10. Which reading skill do you do best?
    a. remember and recognize details and the correct order of events
    b. recognize the main idea and imagine how the characters feel

11. The notes you take from a lecture or the book are
    a. very well organized, perhaps even in outline form, with many words on a page.
    b. scribbled all over the page with arrows and doodles, with words and phrases instead of clauses and sentences.

Count your *a*'s and *b*'s and record your results (a-5, b-3, for example). You can count the number of stars, or *both*'s, you indicated, too. Remember, this is not a scientifically precise test. It is an informal test to open your mind so you can understand your own learning style(s).

Answering more *a*'s means your "left brain" is probably dominant. Dominant here means that you use more of your left brain's skills or that you use them more often for problem-solving and learning. In general, the left brain is verbal, analytic, linear, logical. It "likes" algebra. It listens to the spoken word very well. It reads very well, especially for details and sequence (linear). It works to keep information orderly, organized. Of course, a left-brain dominant person is going to read all the instructions first. It's verbal and logical. It will always take a paragraph over a diagram. Students who are left-brain dominant should sit on the left because they are more aware of what is going on to their right.

If you chose more *b*'s, you are probably right-brain dominant. The right hemisphere is visuo-spatial (space). It can "see" and match visual patterns very well. It draws well because it controls movement through space and sees lines better than the left brain. The right brain is emotional and "dreamy." It is holistic: it sees the pattern, problem, information as a whole.

The right-brain dominant student may understand the main idea of a story but not know exactly why she is correct because it doesn't perceive details as well as the left brain. Of course, the right brain "wants" to see and touch the parts before it allows the left brain to read the instructions. Lines like those in diagrams and drawings are read well by the right brain, which "likes" geometry. Study the selected list of strengths and skills of the left and right hemispheres to imagine how your "brains" work together and what you might do to improve how the brain works. Right-brain dominant students should sit on the right because they are more aware of what is going on to their left.

If you wanted to mark both a and b most often, you may be using the skills of both sides of your brain equally well. In that case, you can try to maintain that equilibrium, that is, avoid the adult lateralization tendency (tendency to use one side of the brain more). However, you may simply be equally weak and incomplete in your use of your brain's powers. You may need to practice "programming" your brain in new ways. You probably need to sit in the middle of the room.

More important than knowing which brain hemisphere is dominant, if that's the case, is understanding how each side assists and completes the other. There is no natural human behavior that one side of the brain can do well without the other.

BRAIN FUNCTIONS[*]

RIGHT HEMISPHERE	LEFT HEMISPHERE
Left ear, eye, side of body	Right ear, eye, side of body
Sense of space to left	Sense of space to right
NON-VERBAL	VERBAL
Symbolism	Grammar
Tone pattern and quality	Analysis of sound
	Syllable recognition
TONAL MEMORY	VERBAL MEMORY
Music—rhythm	Sequence of tones
Pitch, Intonation, Melody	

---

[*] Adapted from Martin Kane, "Cognitive Styles of Thinking and Learning: Part One," *Academic Therapy* 19:5 May, 1984.

EMOTIONAL thought	RATIONAL thought
Emotional aspects of words and pictures	Recognition of meaning of words and pictures
Laughing, crying	Analysis of words, pictures
Creative language	Labels space
Sense of space, movement	Notes, details
Drawing	Sees printed words and letters
Inductive	Deductive
Divergent	Convergent
Holistic	Analytical
Intuitive, simultaneous	Linear
Visuo-spatial	Logical
Direction/Location	(verbal/analytic)
Concrete	
RELATIONAL Concepts	SEQUENTIAL Concepts
Geometric	Algebraic
Passive	Aggressive
Feminine	Masculine
Mysterious	Active
Artistic	

What does all of this mean? For one thing, it means that you may need to identify the side of the brain (more accurately, the skills associated with it) you neglect to stimulate, to use properly. It means that if you consistently fail vocabulary tests in which memorization is necessary, for example, you may be relying heavily on your "left brain," which processes words better. You may need to put your right brain on the job by giving it pictures to connect with the words or concepts you are trying to learn/memorize. It may mean that when you take notes on complicated subjects, not just facts but facts that add up to an idea, a generalization, a theory, you should not put the ideas in an outline which is appealing and understandable mainly to the left brain because it is linear. Perhaps you should take notes more in picture or diagram form, arranging the words and phrases so that you can see their relation to each other.

It also means that when you read a story you should invite yourself to imagine being in the story. Stories, poems, plays, and even non-fiction works like histories are full of pictures, sounds, smells, feelings. Imagining what the streets, buildings, conquerors, generals, battles, etc. look, sound, smell, feel like is part of the reading process, but many "poor" or uninterested readers neglect this essential but non-verbal, less conscious aspect of reading. They read for information but do not let the information get fully inside their heads.

If you neglect your left brain as many other poor readers do, you may be the best student in the class at understanding the theme of a story. But you may not be able to pass a reading test because you forget all those details. You might recognize that you are not a "detail person," and make a habit of returning to the story to check details. You may need to make a mental picture of such details so your dominant right brain will help your left remember those details.

Two of the greatest "studiers" of all time were Leonardo da Vinci and Albert Einstein. Brain researchers tell us that the main difference between da Vinci and Einstein and the rest of us ordinary folk may be that they developed both sides of the brain equally well. Da Vinci's notebooks offer evidence of this. Tony Buzan,[*] a leading learning expert, cites the "cross-over" of left and right brain talents in Da Vinci's work. In his scientific notebooks, there are many drawings and images. In his art notebooks, there are many mathematical and scientific figures. But the most startling example of "whole brain" success that Buzan gives is that of Albert Einstein. Most of us don't understand

---

[*] Tony Buzan, *Use Both Sides of Your Brain*. New York: Dutton, 1983.

his famous Theory of Relativity, but we know he is a very famous scientist whose work has resulted in many "miracles" of modern science such as space travel. We imagine that Einstein was very good at mathematics and that he arrived at his Theory of Relativity through long hours over mathematical figures and formulas. Actually, Einstein failed mathematics in school and was interested in such right-dominant activities as violin playing, art, sailing, and imagination games.

In fact, Einstein was playing an imagination game when he conceived his most famous scientific theory. He imagined riding sunbeams to the ends of the universe. When he found himself returning to the sun, he realized that space was curved. Then he used mathematic and scientific calculations and words to describe this universe he had imagined. It took a synthesis of the talents of his left and right hemispheres for him to succeed.

What has all this got to do with you and studying? Da Vinci's and Einstein's success suggests that the secret to understanding and learning anything lies not so much in what we were born with but in using what we are all born with *fully*. So our objectives are to understand how the brain learns best and to apply that understanding to the development of our own study skills.

Let's look at the facts about remembering first because memorization is what much of studying is about. Often you have understood the facts when they were presented to you, but you forgot the details by the time test day came around.

Consider the following facts about memory.
1. You remember best the information from the beginning and end of a presentation, whether it's a list of words or a lecture on a complex theory.
2. Your recall (ability to remember what you've learned) is highest in the moments right after you've learned the new material. The brain is still

"working" on the material. It is still integrating the new information—linking it to information already stored—making new connections. After that, without carefully timed review, recall falls off quickly and drastically.

3. Without review you forget 80 percent of the details you have learned by the end of the first 24-hour period.
4. You remember items better when they are associated by repetition, sense, and exaggeration.

REPETITION

Remember that the brain learns in different ways. The left brain learns best by hearing, reading, and speaking words. The right brain learns best by seeing pictures and patterns and by doing. You may learn—or feel you learn—by only one method, but why take chances? If remembering something is important, you can cover all the bases by reading it aloud, discussing the information with others or having someone repeat it aloud for you, forming pictures in your mind, writing the material—quickly but repeatedly.

SENSE

The brain learns new material best when it is associated with something else. Use associating pictures, sounds (rhyme), and other sense associations to allow the brain to make links between former experience and new experience so the new will be remembered. (You might use smell in chemistry, for example.)

EXAGGERATION

Make your associations as wild as possible. Tony Buzan suggests the following types of associations:

       a. Absurdities/exaggerations

       b. Sex

       c. Movement

       d. Color

(Don't make the associations too complicated. You don't want to remember the association and forget the fact.)

- Understanding and recall work together best if accompanied by breaks after learning periods of 20 to 40 minutes. Less than 20 minutes does not give the brain time to integrate the material. After about 40 minutes your brain needs time to deal with the information. Material learned after that will probably be forgotten immediately.

- The breaks do not need to be long. The brief breaks are especially important for capturing the information learned in the middle of the process, the part you are most likely to forget.

  Note: A break can be just changing activities. Drawing a map is a break from reading or doing math problems, but you need to change positions or stand for a moment—relax your body.

- When you have truly learned something so you can recall it on command, the memory of that item has actually "laid tracks" on your brain. Researchers have discovered that the brain's chemical system lays a film or track on nerve cells when something is important and/or repeated often enough. It may also be stored in special Long Term Memory Centers or pathways—they aren't sure yet—but your brain is physically altered in the remembering process. Repetition and association insure this physical alteration.

- As we saw earlier, the brain learns best things which are associated with other things. It is much more effective to "slot" details into an overall picture of all the associated details and ideas than to study something by itself. If at all possible, study information in the form of a Mind Map (key words connected with lines to other key words). Study details with reference to other details.

The facts above suggest a program for developing recall, for insuring that you remember the information learned:

- First, review should take place about 10 minutes after the first learning session of one hour or less. The review should take about 10 minutes. This maintains recall for about 24 hours.
- The next review should take place at the end of the first 24-hour period and should last 2-4 minutes. Recall will be retained for about a week.
- Another 2-minute review should occur after that week.
- Review again for a few minutes after a month. The memory will then have "laid a track" on your brain and will be stored in Long Term Memory.

As I mentioned earlier, there has been criticism of the left-brain, right-brain dichotomy from researchers. Just when educators were beginning to use the information, scientists said, "Whoa. We're going too far with this." Some educators and researchers were "pigeon-holing" people as either left-brained or right-brained (giving the impression that people were exclusively one or the other) and personality-typing according to brain dominance. Although the different areas of the brain are responsible for different functions, not all people have the same functions in the same area. For instance, seventy percent of left-handed people may have the verbal and analytical skills in the right or frontal area of the brain. So, educators backed off the left-brain, right-brain distinction and started talking about students as being predominantly "global" or "analytical." *Global* refers to relying more on holistic, intuitive, emotional, and creative skills, and *analytical* refers to relying more on details and logical reasoning.

Rita and Kenneth Dunn have done extensive research in the area of learning styles. She describes her husband as a global learner/writer who can sprawl out on the sofa with snack food, television, and interruptions and produce work on a paper while she sits upstairs alone in a straight-back chair to produce. Together they have written many articles and have developed an instrument for assessing learning style preferences in students.

The National Association of Secondary School Principals has also developed a learning style assessment instrument for use in schools. The idea is to match students' learning styles with the way they are taught. As you may have guessed, most of the teaching that goes on in the public schools, especially in junior and senior high, appeals to the talents of the left hemisphere. The goal now is to encourage teachers to use strategies that appeal to global learners, those who learn best through seeing (visual) and/or touching and doing (kinetic), in addition to appealing to auditory learners.

Many books are available to help students, writers, and artists use the skills of both sides to the fullest. The main thing is to recognize that the talents of both sides can be enhanced. When I first read about brain functions, I knew immediately that I was "left-dominant," or analytical. I understood why I was put off by Macintosh computers, for instance, with the icons instead of words. I related the information to my own experience; it made sense. Now (after Diane's prodding), I do things to stimulate the right hemisphere, such as using colored highlighters on my lists.

Reading

If you are already a student of life, you probably read everything you can get your hands on from the cereal box as you are eating breakfast to the newspaper to selected magazines and books. Some experts seem to think that readers are a dying breed in this world of visual images, and that may be so to an extent. Kids today spend much more time in front of television sets and computers (playing games) than they do curled up with good books.

When we were young and didn't have 49 channels of visual blitz from which to select, we escaped, traveled, solved mysteries, and had wild adventures via books. I remember moving from the Trixie Beldon series to Nancy Drew in the fifth grade. In the sixth and seventh grades, I read the entire Perry Mason series, borrowed one at a time from a neighbor. When I was in high school, I read Leon Uris, and later, I read everything from *Cosmopolitan* magazine to books such as *The Great Pyramid*. Now I read *Harper's*, *Atlantic Monthly*, *Newsweek*, political magazines with both left- and right-wing perspectives, and nonfiction books on current affairs. That's all for fun—to satisfy my brain and to know what's going on. I rarely read fiction. But that's *my* preference. I have a friend who reads historical romances. My friend learns from well-written historical romances and finds great pleasure in reading. Her love of reading gave her a jump start as an adult student; her independent reading had helped prepare her for college reading. College reading assignments offered pleasure, not pain.

Can you get through college if you don't like to read? Sure. Many do. Many students read only what they have to read and take every short-cut possible and manage to make A's. But *getting by* and *getting the most* from college are different. You might say that *getting by* is pleasing the teacher, playing the game, and getting a diploma, and *getting the most* is pleasing yourself, being a real student, and getting an education. If you already love to read, you are halfway there. If you don't like to read, try to discover why you don't and remedy the situation. Below are some possibilities:

1. **When you read, you get eye-strain and/or a headache.**

   Remedy: Have your eyes examined. If you are over 40 and are normal, you may need reading glasses. I use the word *normal* because most people, even if they have never worn glasses, develop presbyopia at about age 40. It is part of the—I hate to say *aging*—process. The adage "You know you're over the hill when your arms aren't long enough to read" is grounded in human biology. If you find yourself moving away from printed material or moving the material away from your eyes in order to focus, you are there. I had perfect vision until age 40. Suddenly—it really seemed to happen overnight—the words on the page were blurry. Like your average paranoiac, I assumed I had a brain tumor. I mentioned my concern to someone who happened to be past 40. The woman told me I probably needed reading glasses and that I could buy them at any drug store. Well, I did the little chart test on the rotating rack at Eckerd's and decided that +1.75 worked well. But later I had a little trouble with them, so when I saw reading glasses at a flea market and heard a woman say, "Why get weak ones? Stronger must be better," I bought a pair of +2.50 glasses. Well, I found out that stronger is not necessarily better. *Right* is better. I went to an optometrist

who said I needed +1.25. Well, he gave me a test—right?
A test. Of course, I had to strain to do my best—right?
Anyway, the strength that is right for me is +1.50. That
will change, I'm sure, and probably I will eventually need
glasses for distance vision also—which means? You
guessed it. Bifocals. So check your vision. The only
people past age 40 who do not need glasses for reading or
other close work are people who start out with something
or another—the opposite—that corrects itself with the
aging process. (See *Prevention* magazine (February, 1990)
for an article on this subject.)

2. **You find it difficult to concentrate on what you are
   reading. You may be (a) so stressed out and circuit-
   overloaded that you find anything challenging too
   much or (b) bored with what you are reading.**

   Remedy a: If you can't concentrate on what you are
   reading because you keep having thoughts about how
   you're going to feed your kids or what your spouse is
   doing in that motel room, it may be that you are going
   through a crisis that makes concentrating on anything
   difficult. In that case, try reading self-help books that
   relate to your situation. These days, books on every
   imaginable personal crisis are available. The reading will
   become relevant to you, and you will be actively seeking
   something from the book. This advice is related to the
   advice for (b) bored readers.

   (Also, many people have found supplements such as
   ginkgo biloba helpful in improving concentration. Exercise
   also stimulates circulation to the brain. Women who think
   they might be going through the change of life can have
   hormone levels checked. An estrogen deficiency might
   result in poor memory and low energy levels.)

Remedy b: Again, read something that is interesting. If you have to start with a novel with a low reading level and fast action and skip over the lengthy description, still you are practicing your reading skills. Reading is like everything else in the world—the more you do it, the better you become at it.

3. **You think your reading skills are poor.**

Remedy: Again, practice reading, and study the sections below.

Mark Twain said that those who *don't* read are no better off than those who *can't* read. Yes, we are becoming a nation of non-readers, but we are paying a price for that. Lower SAT scores may be a result of decreased emphasis on reading. At any rate, IQ scores in adults are related to reading. Do smarter people read, or do readers become smarter? I don't know. But I believe it is very important to foster a love of reading in children. One way to do this is to take kids to the library and make a big deal of the privilege of reading books and/or to buy books for kids, or better yet, let kids buy books with their own money. They will read them. If you want to feel guilty as hell about taking books for granted, read Richard Wright's essay about how he checked out books in the name of his white employer and taught himself to read. (At that time, it was illegal to teach African-Americans to read.)

Another way the lack of reading affects today's kids is in a loss of imagination. A reader uses mental skills to conjure up images as she reads.

She sees the protagonist, hears the crowd roar, etc. But television and movies provide those images. Today, even the images evoked by a favorite song are provided by MTV.

We're losing something, and we may not fully understand the consequences until it is too late.

Varying reading rates

Different kinds of material can be read at different speeds. The trick is to know what you want from the material and get it. If you are reading a light, escape novel—a romance or mystery, perhaps, you may want to read fast, going mainly for the action. And you may even skip some descriptive details, for instance. There is no crime in judicious skipping of boring sections. The author's pet interest may not be yours, and you are not under contract to read every word. On the other hand, much of the great literature should be read slowly. The language of the past takes a little more attention to understand. Also, the works of master writers are so rich that a fast reading misses much of what makes the writer great. For instance, (again) I'm a Mark Twain fan. I especially enjoy his social writings, and I read them slowly, sometimes rereading a sentence that is especially artful. I don't want to miss a single word because a single word or the placement of a word in a sentence can make me smile or recall associations or draw conclusions or have ideas for my own writing. Many works of literature may be read again and again and still hold surprises and new insights for the reader with each reading. The pleasure in reading good literature comes not from knowing what will happen next but from the *experience* of reading, from the way the words are linked together, from the images evoked by the metaphors and similes, and from the feelings we get. Reading good literature is something to be savored, not gulped.

Also very technical material, the kind of material you will be reading in textbooks, should be read slowly. You might need to reread some of the material to understand it thoroughly before you go on. Other reading material can be skimmed quickly for key words and concepts. These are tips for reading technical material:

1. Do *not* begin reading at page 1 and continue straight through to the last page.

2. Before you read a single page, do three things:
    a. Jot down everything or anything you know about the subject, no matter how little you know. This provides a context for the new material.
    b. Get an overview of the material. Flip through the entire chapter, book, whatever. Glance at the boldfaced headings and skim contents. Skimming is the student's best friend. (See SQ3R below.)
    c. Ask yourself what your goals are—what you expect to be able to do or know after studying. Write down a list of questions to be answered with your reading.

These activities ready the brain for the new information. They call up stored information and allow associations to be made. Much of your careful reading will be in vain without these readiness activities. Also, you will have defined the limits of the task. Expectation is an important element of learning.

3. Don't take notes page by page. Read a section or all of the material, and then jot down key concepts (in single words) right after you have finished reading. You will not have the whole picture until you've read it all. Then when you write notes you will be
    a. slotting the information into the whole picture—the best way for your brain to take it in, and

b. you will be repeating something that has associations.

4. If at all possible, mark the study material. Use straight and wavy lines in the margin by important material. Highlight with color.

5. Remember to take timed breaks after 20 to 40 minutes of reading/studying. If your study period is going to be interrupted by longer breaks, before you leave the material for hours/days, do your jotting. Go over your notes for a few minutes before you begin again—you will ready your brain again just like you did in the beginning. If you didn't take notes—perhaps you didn't know you were going to be interrupted—jot down everything you remember before resuming reading.

6. You may worry that your first "jottings" are not complete. After all, if you had perfect recall, you wouldn't need to develop study techniques, would you? After making your first notes quickly without referring to the book, then you can return to the material and add significant details. At this stage you should be able to recall the material for a test in the next 24 hours.

7. Leave it. Come back to your notes a day later. Rewrite your notes quickly. Spend a few minutes rewriting and studying your notes.

8. About one week later, return to your notes, rewrite them and study them briefly.

Note: If your study material includes diagrams and graphs, use your finger or a pen/pencil to guide your eye as you study the lines.

The study environment

The environment you choose for studying is important. Find a place that offers some freedom from distractions. If there are distracting noises, soft background music can drown out some of the chaos in the next room or outside. If you try to study while lying in bed, you are likely to fall asleep before you have finished the assignment. Sitting in a comfortable chair puts enough tension on the muscles to keep one awake.

Making a chart or list of your assignments and setting aside a block of time for each one will help you keep from feeling overwhelmed and will also help assure that you don't devote all of your available time to one subject while neglecting the others.

The SQ3R study technique

The SQ3R method has been around since 1946 when Francis Robinson published *Effective Study*. To develop the habit of using the technique when you study, you might make a sign with the key words *survey, question, read, recite,* and *review* and post the sign in your study area as a reminder.

1. **Survey** the reading material, looking at headings, boldfaced or italicized words, charts and graphs, and summaries.

2. **Question**. Write down questions you expect to have answered in the text. These questions can be made by turning the headings and boldfaced words into questions.

(Example heading: The Spanish-American War. Example questions: When was the Spanish-American War? What started the war? Why was it fought? Where was it fought? What were the results of the war?

3. **Read** the material one section at a time.

4. **Recite** the answers to the questions you have written as you read the material. Try to put answers in your own words. This may involve writing notes in your own words. The act of writing itself helps the writer remember material. In one study, students were given a lecture. Half the students were allowed to take notes; the other half did not take notes. The notes were taken from the students after the lecture session. Later, the students who did not take notes were given a sheet to review briefly, but the students who took notes were not given review sheets. When the two groups of students were tested, it was discovered that the students who took notes on the original lecture had retained more than the students who did not take notes but were given review sheets.

   Ludy Gibson took few notes in class but tape-recorded the lectures. Later, she would write out notes as she listened to the tapes. Listening well in class and reinforcing what she heard by listening again and writing notes worked for her. She said she was ready for tests after only a brief review.

5. **Review** the material by looking over questions and recalling answers.

Using the SQ3R technique will take some effort at first. You must, for instance, train your eyes to look for the important details as you survey. Learning to skim and scan for information is especially important to students. You don't have time to wade through dull prose when you are trying to prepare for a test.

Readability levels

If you decide to choose education as a field, you will learn about readability formulas. These formulas use different aspects of written text (number of syllables in a passage, number of words in sentences, etc.) to determine the reading level. But aside from learning about readability levels for the purpose of choosing texts for children to read, you will notice that some textbooks are easier to read than others. In other words, the same material can be presented in a way that is accessible to a reader with a certain level of skill or presented—figuratively anyway—as Greek. The textbook used in an undergraduate psychology course I took years ago was practically unreadable. Other students in the class complained about the book and thought the course was especially hard because of the text. I had been introduced to Fry's readability formula in an education course, so I tested several passages from the psychology text. The book registered off the scale. The book was far beyond college level, not because it was so well written but because it was poorly written. Good writing is readable.

If you end up with a text that is very hard to read, try checking out a text on the same subject at the library. You may find the same information presented in a more readable form. One woman was having fits trying to read Chaucer in Old English. She finally checked out a Modern English translation and was then able to enjoy reading *The Canterbury Tales*.

Note: You can check the readability level of your own writing with a word processing program such as MS Word.

Developing vocabulary

Unfamiliar words can slow down the reading process. Looking up every unfamiliar word in the dictionary is usually not good. I say *usually* because it is necessary to know the meaning of key words and concepts. Usually these terms are explained in the text, but if they aren't, you will want to look them up in order to understand the rest of the material. The vocabulary used in the different fields is often referred to as a language in itself. If, for instance, you want to understand the instructor in a math class, you must understand math language. Otherwise, the important concepts will go right over your head. Most textbooks have glossaries in the back that give related terms and definitions. When you enroll in a course and get the textbook, you might make reading through the glossary a priority, something you do before you begin your first reading assignment.

Often you can determine the meaning of an unfamiliar word by using context clues, clues from the material surrounding the word. The following is a list of context clues to look for when deciphering the meaning of unfamiliar words:

1. **Examples of the unfamiliar word**
   He is *ambidextrous*. He uses his left hand for writing, but he uses his right hand for eating and pitching.

2. **Definitions and restatements**
   The issue was suddenly *ubiquitous*; it was everywhere. Every talk show featured it, and new books on the issue were coming out daily.

3. **Cause and Effect clues**
   Because she had passed the test, she felt *elated*.

4. **Synonyms**
    (clues that indicate a word is similar in meaning to a familiar word) She *evinced*, or showed, her determination to get a diploma.

5. **Antonyms**
    (clues that indicate an unfamiliar word has a meaning opposite a familiar word or phrase) Instead of being flexible about the possibility, she was *adamant* that she would not take a course that involved cutting up worms.

    You can build your vocabulary through reading. You may want to keep a list of new words as you run across them. You can look them up later, study the meaning, and add the word to your vocabulary by using it several times in different sentences to reinforce learning.

Using mnemonics

Memory aids include acronyms, words formed from first letters (i.e., NATO = North Atlantic Treaty Organization). You can make your own words from first letters of lists of facts. You can also make your own sentences from first letters, or find out standard study aids such as the following sentence that includes first letters of the planets: Mary's Violet Eyes Make John Stay UP Nights (Mercury, Venus, Earth, Mars, Jupiter, Saturn, Uranus, Pluto, Neptune)

Taking lecture notes

Reading the chapter beforehand helps prepare your brain to take in the new information during a lecture. Be sure you understand all the terms in the chapter and write out definitions in your own words. What the instructor says will make sense if you have prepared well.

When you take notes during a lecture, don't try to write everything down. As mentioned before, writing only key words can help you recall what was said and still allow you to really listen to the lecturer. But be careful that you don't end up with notes that mean nothing to you when you actually begin to study. Sometimes shorthand notations are useless after the material is cold. (This is another good reason to review your notes immediately after the class and fill in things you remember and make additional notes.

You might also write in your notes personal words or phrases that help you associate the concept mentioned by the teacher to something in your life. You might also include your rational or emotional reactions to the material, such as "b.s." or stars, underlining, and exclamation points for important concepts. And try to translate as much as possible to your own language. Making these mental translations and responding to information helps you listen actively. Active listening may even involve "living" the material. For instance, during a science discussion of anthracite coal, BE the coal and make up a story with its characteristics personified: A day in the life of anthracite coal.

The art of note taking involves writing neither too little nor too much. If you try to write everything, note taking becomes the end rather than the means. If the professor gives so much new information it seems impossible to write enough, ask whether his or her lecture notes are available in the library or bring a tape recorder to class.

After you have taken the first test for each instructor, you will know more about what and how to study for future tests. You may find that the one thing you passed over when studying (because you didn't understand it or because it seemed irrelevant or boring) will be the first thing on the test. (Some instructors have old tests on file that you can go over to get an idea of the kinds of information the instructor considers important.)

Study groups

Giving and receiving information orally helps reinforce it in the brain (remember the chemical tracks?). If you can spare the time to meet with one or more people from your class to study, it will probably pay off. I say *probably* because there is always the danger that you will be used and end up giving far more than you get. But if you can find even a friend with whom to trade copies of notes, you will get another interpretation of the material and perhaps information that you missed.

Making tests as study aids

Making up your own tests can help you prepare for the real thing. You can use the questions in the back of the chapter and additional information from your lecture notes to make questions to answer. Just the process of making the tests will help you study. You may want to focus on the things you had more trouble remembering.

In a graduate statistics course, after the second of three tests, the woman beside me showed me the test she had made to study. It was almost word-for-word the test we had just taken. My first thought was that she had cheated, that she had acquired a copy of the test beforehand. "His test are from his review," she said. I looked back at the review, and she was right. He simply omitted words from the review statements for a fill-in-the-blank test that, from my perspective, measured whether a student had talked to other students who had taken his courses or, perhaps, whether a student was real perceptive. I had studied all the material, and I knew it. I did not, however, know many of the odd words he had omitted. The savvy woman who had made her own test did.

The study environment and test day

A comfortable study environment is important. A tight waistband or pinched toe can be distracting when studying or, later, when taking a test. In fact, on test day, try to recreate your study environment in some way. One student told me she studies in a comfortable sweat suit and wears the same sweats on test day. If you smoke, you may want to take nicotine gum on test day and a straw or some facsimile of a cigarette to hold in one hand.

Further notes

Many people find the video "Where There's A Will, There's an A" helpful. You can probably find it in the library or in the academic advisement or student services office.

Also, remember to allow study time for each subject as you go. In other words, don't wait until the night before the test to cram. After you have studied, however, you will want to go over your study notes immediately before a test. If you made notes on the material you had a hard time remembering, you can put the information in the front of your brain right before the test and have a better chance of recall.

Chapter 7
Quick English Review

The review included in this chapter is adapted from a hand-out I prepared after a couple of students asked for a kind of "cheat sheet" that was concise enough to memorize. The examples are simple. (For more intensive help with writing, see Chapter 8 on the writing process or any number of writing textbooks, including *The Informed Citizen: Argument and Analysis*). Start your review of the conventions of written English by taking the quiz below. Chances are you will start recalling the rules you memorized in school. If you didn't internalize the rules then, now is a good time to do so. They don't change, and they will serve you for the rest of your life.

Quiz

The following sentences have one or more mistakes in grammar, usage, or mechanics. After you determine what you think is wrong in each sentence, read the explanation that follows.

1. By the Wednesday before the plans were set.
2. Do not misunderstand me, he was not like most juveniles.
3. I don't know whether or not she and her family is willing to pay the price.

4. Knowing inside yourself that you have helped someone learn something useful, is a great reward.
5. One who you can tell your deepest secrets to without a worry.
6. She lives in Lumberton north Carolina.
7. During the six months of modeling school I went through a metamorphosis.
8. The costs of education is rising.
9. Sometimes a person loses sight of their original purpose.
10. The natural environment is choked by this pollutant as well as the individual.

Answers/Explanations

1. (Not a complete sentence) What happens *by the Wednesday before the plans were set*? We don't know. Instead of a complete sentence, we have an adverbial clause telling *when* something happened, but we don't know what happened.
2. (Run-on) Two complete thoughts are combined with a comma. Although we can combine two thoughts with a comma and a conjunction (*and, but, or*), we can't just use a comma. In this case, we need a semicolon or a period and capital letter to make two separate sentences.
3. (Subject/verb agreement error) *She and her family* is a plural subject and must have the plural verb are.
4. (Comma splice) We don't separate a subject and a verb with a single comma. *Knowing inside yourself that you have helped someone learn something useful* is the complete subject; the verb is *is*.
5. (Another "frag.," incomplete sentence) *Who* is the *one you can tell your deepest secrets to without a worry.*

6. (Comma and capitalization error) Put a comma between Lumberton and North Carolina. Capitalize proper names (North Carolina).

7. (Comma needed after *school*) *During the six months of modeling school* is an introductory adverbial clause telling *when*. It should be separated from the main part of the sentence with a comma.

8. (Subject/verb agreement error) *Costs* is plural and needs the plural verb are. Agreement in this case could also be achieved by eliminating the *s* in *costs* and keeping the singular verb *is*.

9. (Pronoun/antecedent error) The pronoun *their* (plural) refers to *a person* (singular). *Their* should be replaced with *his or her*.

10. (Misplaced phrase confuses the meaning) The sentence actually says that the pollutant and the individual both choke the natural environment. The sentence should read: The natural environment as well as the individual are choked by this pollutant.

A quick review

Now that you have refreshed your memory (and probably discovered that you remembered far more than you thought), read over the following sections. The Parts of Speech information is included mainly to refresh your memory so that the terms can be used in explanations. The rules of punctuation and usage, however, are important. Memorizing these few simple rules can save you a lot of frustration when you write. Remember, you don't need to worry about correctness until you are in the editing and proofreading stages of the writing process (see Chapter 8).

Nouns—name a person, place, thing, or idea

Proper nouns name a specific person, place, or thing and are capitalized: John, Grand Canyon, St. Louis, Department of Defense.

Common nouns are not capitalized: boy, the canyon, a city, a government agency.

Nouns can be used as subjects or objects:
Sue (subject) gave the dress (object) to Ellen (object of preposition).

Verbs— show action or state of being

Action—*walk, laugh, fly*
State of being—*is, are, was, am*
Some verbs are used as helpers, or auxiliary, verbs— *has, have, will, was.*

Verbs have tenses that serve as a kind of road map through time:
Mary *works* today. (present)
Linda *worked* yesterday. (past)
Linda *has worked* many times in the past. (past participle)
Mary *will work* today (future perfect)

Things to remember about nouns and verbs:

The subject and *present tense* verb of a sentence must be in agreement:

Singular subjects have singular verbs, and singular verbs end in *s*. (Note the *s* on the word *drive* in *Mary drives today*.)
He runs. (*He* is singular.)
They run. (*They* is plural.)

You run. (Well, sorry folks, here is a slight oddity. The second person pronoun *you* works like a plural whether it applies to one person or several.)

A complete sentence must have a subject (a noun or noun phrase) and a verb: *Linda worked yesterday*.

A complete sentence must represent a complete thought (called an independent clause because it can stand alone):

Because Linda worked yesterday has a noun and a verb, but we do not have a complete sentence. Something else is needed to complete the meaning of the words.

Because Linda worked yesterday, Mary works today.

Now we have a dependent clause with a subject and verb and an independent clause that can stand alone. The subject of the sentence is *Mary*; the main verb is *works*.

So far, so good? Is it starting to come back, now? Of course, you know all of this. You use these subjects and verbs, dependent and independent clauses constantly in speech. The only thing you need is a memory jogger, and I promise to keep this section brief.

–One more thing about subjects and verbs . . .

Passive and Active Voice—It is usually best to use active voice when writing: The (subject) did something (verb) to something (object).

The umpire called the foul ball.

In passive voice, the object (foul ball) becomes the subject: *The foul ball was called by the umpire*. The active voice sentence contains fewer words and is more direct than the passive sentence.

When editing, look for forms of the verb *be* (*is, was, am*) as clues to passive sentence construction, then decide whether you should change the passive sentence to active voice. There *are* good reasons and appropriate times to use passive voice:

1. **The doer of the action is understood or unimportant**
    Example: *The letter was delivered yesterday.* (It is understood that someone delivered the letter; we don't care who did that. The important thing is *when* the letter was delivered.)

2. **When you want to avoid placing blame or the actor is unknown**
    Example: *The error was made in the accounting department.* (We could say "An accounting clerk made the error," but we can avoid direct blame by using passing voice.)

–One more thing about verbs . . .

We talked briefly about verb tenses. Most English words form their past and past participle forms by adding *-d* or *-ed*. But remember the list of irregular verbs in your grade school grammar book? The irregular verbs form their past and past participle tenses by:

1. changing vowels
    He runs. (present)
    He ran. (past)
    He has run. (past participle)
2. changing vowels and endings (-en)
    He drives. (present)
    He drove. (past)
    He has driven (past participle)
3. changing word forms completely
    He does it. (present)

He did it. (past)
He has done it before. (past participle)

Troublesome Verbs

Lie (to rest) and Lay (to put or place)

Memory tip: People lie.
She will lie in the sun.
She lay in the sun yesterday.
She has lain in the sun many times.

Chickens lay. (put eggs in the nest)
The chicken will lay an egg. (I will lay the paper on the desk.)
The chicken laid an egg. (I laid the paper on the desk.)
The chicken has laid many eggs. (I have laid the paper on the desk many times in the past.)

Sit (to take a seat) and Set (to place)

Memory tip: People sit.
Please sit down.
People sat quietly by the window.
People have sat for hours.
Objects are placed.
She sets the vase on the table now.
(Remember the -*s* for singular/present tense verbs.)
She set the vase on the table yesterday.
She has set the vase on the table many times in the past.

Rise (to stand up) and Raise (to lift up)

Memory tip: All rise and raise the window.

Most importantly, **maintain tense consistency when writing.**
The following passage will illustrate the kind of confusion that results from inconsistent tenses:

Jack and Jill ran up the hill. They fetch a pail of water. Jack had fallen down and breaks his crown, and Jill came tumbling after.

When did this unfortunate episode happen?
Is it happening now? (fetch, breaks)
Did it happen in the recent past? (ran, came)
Did it happen in the distant past? (had fallen)

I mentioned before that verb tenses serve the reader as a kind of road map through time. When proofreading, check to make sure that verb tenses are consistent. For most writing you will probably use past tense verbs most of the time with occasional past participle verbs.

Exception: We sometimes use what is called the historical present when discussing works of literature: In the innocent boy Huckleberry Finn, Twain creates a complex character who gives the reader not only the joy of laughter but also food for thought.

Pronoun—replaces nouns and must agree with antecedents (the words replaced) in number

I, me, mine— first person/singular
We, us— first person/plural
You, yours— second person/singular and plural

He, him, she, her, it— third person/singular
They, them— third person/plural

Although you probably don't stop and think about it very often, you have internalized these constructions if you are a native English speaker. You know which form goes in the subject position and which form goes in the object position: *I* (subject) want it. Give it to *me* (object). *He* (subject) did it. It was done to *him* (object), etc. When you were two years old, you might have said something like, "Me want milk," but by the time you were four, you had internalized the correct grammatical construction, " I want milk"—all without the help of an English teacher. Native speakers of English make few grammatical errors, although they may make usage errors, such as using the wrong verb form (*He run up the hill* or *between you and I*). To check compound structures, eliminate the first part: *between* is a preposition, and the nouns that follow are objects. You wouldn't follow a preposition such as *above* or *on* with the word *I* (*above I, between I*) so the correct usage is *between you and me*.

Native speakers also might make the mistake of using an objective pronoun in the nominative (subject) place (*Them don't look right*) or of using a pronoun that doesn't agree with its antecedent. One of the most common involves the words *everyone* and *everybody*, two words that are always singular but often used to refer to a group:

Everyone should keep their coats on.
    should be
Everyone should keep his or her coat on.

Preposition— the little words that we were told don't belong at the end of a sentence, but which sometimes find themselves there.

Churchill's famous debunking of that idea is " up with which I will not put." Avoiding prepositions at the ends of sentences results in a formal style that may in some cases be unsatisfactory. For instance, in this book you will find ending prepositions because I wanted to keep the style informal. For instance, when the ending preposition is eliminated in *You may find a friend to exchange notes with*, it becomes the more formal *You may find a friend with whom to exchange notes.* Also, we have many two-word verbs today, and they often end up at the end of a sentence: *He will stand up.*

What we want to avoid are unnecessary prepositions at the end of sentences: *Where are you at?* should be simply *Where are you?* Usage errors are sometimes peculiar to a regional dialect.

Memory Tip: You might think of prepositions as anything a squirrel can do to a tree: run up a tree, down a tree, beside a tree, in a tree, by a tree, along a tree, etc. (Main exception: *of*)

One other note about prepositions— you never find the subject of a sentence in a prepositional phrase. If you are checking the subject verb agreement in a sentence, eliminate the prepositional phrases to find the subject, then check to make sure the verb agrees with it:
The habit of the people of the cities by the lakes was to rise early in the morning.

After the prepositional phrases are eliminated it becomes clear that *habit* (singular) is the subject, so the verb (*was*) must be singular.

Adjective—modifies nouns and pronouns (a *red* car, a *wild* horse)

Adverb—modifies verbs and other adverbs (*strongly recommend, spoke very frankly*); gives information about when, how, or to what degree.

Memory Tip: most adverbs have an *-ly* ending. The same words might be used as adjectives without the *-ly* ending (a *frank* speech, a *strong* recommendation).

Article—*a, an, the* (akin to the adjective)

These words give native speakers almost no problem except an occasional *a/an* confusion. The article does, however, present problems for some speakers of English as a second language.

Rule: *A* precedes a consonant sound (a vehicle, a house); *an* precedes a vowel sound (an orange, an eagle).

Exception: *An historian* is about the only survivor of the *an* for *h* sound, and it is mainly used in formal writing or speaking. This comes from the British silent *h*; *hour* is one silent *h* word; consequently, we say *an* hour. Remember that the sound is important, not whether the first letter is a vowel or a consonant.

Interjections—Exclamatory words that often come at the beginning of sentences and are usually followed by commas

Example: *Oh, I didn't know that.*

Now, that really wasn't so painful, and I'll bet you remembered much more than you thought you would. Keep in mind that I discuss the parts of speech only because I will refer to them in discussions about writing. That means that you don't need to practice parsing (identifying parts of speech) or diagramming sentences. You will not be asked to do that in college. In fact, enlightened educators frown on both activities because they take time away from actual writing practice. Students do need to know something about grammar but should be taught in the context of their own writing.

Punctuation

The biggest problem students have with punctuation is deciding where and when to use commas. When put in proper context, however, the comma problem can be handled fairly easily. That is not to say that you will never again have a question about comma usage, but at least you can minimize the problems by memorizing four simple rules.

Commas

Rule 1:   **Use a comma to separate items in a series and dates, between cities and states, between a name and a title, and between an interjection and a sentence.**

Example 1:   We had ham, eggs, toast, and orange juice for breakfast.

(The last comma—before *and*— is optional but preferred in formal writing. You might want to get in the habit of using it.)

Example 2:   Jacob was born March 7, 1996.

Note: The example above is a *simple sentence*; it contains one independent clause.

Example 3:   We wanted to go to St. Louis, Missouri, but we took a wrong turn and ended up in Memphis, Tennessee.

Note: The example sentence is a *compound sentence*; it contains more than one independent clause.

Example 4:   Because it is an important meeting, John Smith, Jr. will attend.

Note: The example is a *complex sentence*; it contains at least one independent clause (John Smith, Jr. will attend) and at least one dependent clause (Because it is an important meeting)

Example 5:   Oops, I fell down.

Rule 2:   **Use a comma to set off nonrestrictive clauses and phrases.**

Okay, perhaps a few definitions are in order.

Clause—collection of words containing a subject and a verb.

Dependent clause—incomplete thought that cannot stand alone as a sentence although it contains a subject and a verb.
   Memory tip: It *depends* on the rest of the sentence.

Independent clause—Complete thought that can stand alone as a sentence.
   Memory tip: *Independent* means "self-reliant."

Nonrestrictive clause—Does not restrict the meaning of the sentence, or is not necessary to the meaning of the sentence.

Example: Jane Smith, who is a very good student, was
absent today.
who is a very good student is the imbedded
nonrestrictive clause.

If we read the sentence without the clause, we have *Jane Smith was absent today*. The meaning of the base sentence is intact; therefore, we set off the nonrestrictive clause (an appositive clause because it defines or identifies Jane Smith) with commas.

Example: All freshmen who fail the test will repeat the
course.
who fail the test is the imbedded clause.

If we read the sentence without the clause, we have *All freshmen will repeat the course*. The meaning here is wrong. Only the freshmen who fail the test will repeat the course, not *all* freshmen. Therefore, *who fail the test* restricts the meaning of the sentence, is vitally important to the sentence, and must be included. We do not use commas to set off restrictive clauses.

Phrase— collection of words without a subject and verb

Example: Jane Smith, a good student, was absent today.
In this case, the inserted information is a
phrase; *a good student* does not have a subject
and a verb.

Rule 3:   **Use a comma to set off an introduction to a
direct quotation.**

Example: Kennedy said, "Ask not what your country can
do for you, but ask what you can do for your
country."

Rule 4:   **Use a comma to separate an introductory clause or a long introductory phrase from the dependent clause.**

Example: When I was young, dinosaurs roamed the earth.
When I was young is an adverbial clause telling when dinosaurs roamed the earth.

Example: If he doesn't straighten up and fly right, he will be sidelined.
If he doesn't straighten up and fly right is a conditional clause.

As for introductory phrases, the rules are not quite so clear-cut. In the old days, the rule was that if the phrase contained four or more words, use a comma. Now, it is permissible to use a comma after any length phrase but necessary for longer ones. So, if you want to be on the safe side, use a comma.

Example: By the gate in the field by the barn, the horse stood. (comma necessary)

Rule 5:   **Use a comma to separate two independent clauses.**

Review definition: Independent Clause—Complete thought that can stand alone as a sentence.

Example: I had a good day, and I decided to celebrate.
I had a good day and *I decided to celebrate* are both complete thoughts or independent clauses (sentences).

There are three ways to treat two adjacent independent clauses:

1. join them with a comma and a *coordinating conjunction* (*and, or, but*) as in the example above
2. join them with a semicolon: I had a good day; I decided to celebrate.
3. separate them (with a period and a capital letter) into two sentences: I had a good day. I decided to celebrate.

Note: The option you choose depends on the relationship of the clauses to each other. If the clauses are not closely related, separate them.

Example: I had a good day. The clock on the wall was ticking.

These two sentences are not closely related enough to join with a comma and conjunction or with a semicolon.

Now you know the basic rules for using commas. If you memorize the rules and stick with them, you can avoid comma splices.

Semicolons

Rule 1:   **Use a semicolon to join two independent clauses.** (discussed above)

Rule 2:   **Use a semicolon to separate items in a series when the items contain commas.**

Example: We decided to meet on November 30, 1998; December 12, 1998; or January 3, 1999.

Note: I have seen many students get in trouble with semicolons. They seemed to have the idea that semicolons were interchangeable with commas. They are not. If you stick to the two uses of semicolons noted above, you will be safe.

Colons

Rule 1:   **Use a colon to show an "as follows" relationship.**

Example: The following items were included in his package: pen, paper, clock, scissors, and tissue.

Rule 2:   **Use a colon to separate hours from minutes when writing the time.**

Example: We left at 1:15 p.m.

End Punctuation

Rule 1:   **Use a period at the end of a declaratory sentence.**
Example: This is easy.

Rule 2:   **Use an exclamation point at the end of exclamatory sentences.**

Example: This is really easy!

Caution: In essay writing, don't try to drive a point home with an exclamation point. Instead, use good, sound support. Exclamation points in essay writing are rare; overuse indicates an immature writing style.

Rule 3:   **Use a question mark at the end of questions.**

Example: Isn't this easy?

Underlining

Rule 1:   **Underline the titles of books, magazines, newspapers, movies, plays, and ships.**

Example: Leon Uris wrote *Mila 18*.

Note: Underlining denotes italics. Printed works use italic type for titles, etc., and with word processing, we can use italics. However, some instructors still prefer underlining.

Quotation Marks

Rule 1:   **Use quotation marks around the titles of poems, songs, chapters in books, and articles in magazines or newspapers.**

Example: Paul Simon wrote the song " Bridge over Troubled Water."

Rule 2:   **Use quotation marks around directly quoted material.**

Example: General Patton said, " When the going gets tough, the tough get going."

Placement of Quotation Marks

Rule 1:   **Periods and commas always go inside quotation marks.**

Example: "He can stay," Susan said, "if he wants to."

Rule 2:   **Colons and semicolons always go outside quotation marks.**

Example: One song from the Sixties is "Get Together"; it is representative of that generation's music.

Rule 3:   **Depending on the sentence, question marks and exclamation points may go either inside or outside the quotation marks. If the entire sentence is a question or exclamation, the question mark is outside.**

Example: Why did she say, "I'll reconsider my answer"?
Example: She asked, "Why?"

Memory tip: Commas and periods, always inside quotation marks; colons and semicolons, always outside marks; question marks and exclamation points—it depends.

Apostrophe

Rule 1:   **Use an apostrophe to replace an omitted letter(s) in a contraction.**

Example: does not; doesn't

Rule 2:   **Use an apostrophe to show possession, or ownership. For singular words, add an apostrophe and -*s*; for plurals ending in -*s*, add only an apostrophe.**

Example: Mary's dress; The boys' gym.

Caution: A common error is to put an apostrophe in *its* when used as a possessive pronoun (i.e., The chicken broke *it's* wing). An apostrophe is used in *its* only when the word is a contraction for *it is* (*it's*).

Commonly Confused Words

Their—possessive pronoun (something belongs to them).

   Memory Tip: Remember the *heir* in *their* to show possession, or remember to write *the* and add *ir*.

They're— contraction for *they are*

   Memory Tip: If you can substitute *they are*, you need *they're*.

There—demonstrative pronoun (Over there— in that place)

   Memory Tip: Remember the *here* in *there* to indicate place.

Your—possessive pronoun (something belongs to you)

You're— contraction for *you are*

Post Quiz

1. Time was ticking away, the biggest event of her senior year was coming.
2. It is the owner's responsibility to train and maintain their animal.
3. We all went to the polling place, vote for a candidate, and returning home after we had finished.
4. Like the pain of my left ankle and the smell of my bloody flesh as it cooked on the still sweltering pavement.
5. As I went out the door she pressed a little woolly white stuffed lamb with black button eyes and a thin navy ribbon around its' neck into my arms which she had just made for her baby.

Answers/Explanations

1. Run-on sentence. This particular pair of sentences could be joined with a semicolon or with a comma and the conjunction *and*. The single comma will not do.
2. Pronoun/antecedent problem. We've have only one owner, so the pronoun must be *he* or *she* instead of *their*.
3. Parallel structure (similar elements should have similar constructions). If we change it to *We all went to the polling place, voted, and returned home after we had finished*, all verbs have the same tense.
4. A frag.! What about these feelings and smells?
5. Misplaced modifier, comma omissions, and incorrect apostrophe. This sentence indicates that the gift-giver had just made the writer's arms for her baby. In fact, unpacking the sentence and separating it into two sentences works best. Corrected version: *As I went out the door, she pressed into my arms a little, woolly, white stuffed lamb*

that she had just made for her baby. The lamb had black button eyes and a thin, navy ribbon around its neck.

Chapter 8

The Writing Process

Many people, when asked what their worst subject in school was, will quickly say, "English." When asked what they disliked most about English class, they will say, "Writing." Actually, most adult students did very little or no writing in school. In the "old" days, *writing* often consisted of filling in blanks in grammar worksheets or diagramming sentences. And when *themes* or *essays* were assigned, it was with little or no instruction on how to go about writing them. Of course, that left the student with the frustrating and grueling task of trying to read the teacher's mind—trying to write a paper that included a generous sprinkling of highfalutin' words.

My theory is those people, in spite of what they say, *don't* hate to write; they just haven't had the opportunity to write in a good situation. In fact, I believe that everyone *loves* to write! You might be thinking now that I'm certifiable, or at least, a brick shy of a load. Okay, let me explain why I believe that everyone loves to write. First of all, everyone has opinions about how things should be, and I've yet to run across a person who doesn't like to express those opinions. We love to tell other people when they are wrong and why they are wrong. We love to lecture kids in hopes they will see the light and avoid the mistakes we made. We love to share our knowledge (recipes, how to ease back pain, etc.) with others.

Writing: Who needs it?

We are social creatures, and we love to communicate. Now, speech is one form of communication, and writing is another. But there are advantages of writing:

1. We can preserve those wonderful thoughts and details.
2. We have a chance to change what we write—to make sure we are saying what we wanted to say.

Writing provides a record of details that are important to a given situation. Suppose the telephone company has billed you for calls to an out-of-country place called Palau. Not only do you not know anyone in Palau, you have never heard of the place and are not even sure how to pronounce it. You pay the bill because you really enjoy the convenience of having a telephone, but you call the phone company and tell them about the mistake. You are assured that you will be given credit. Well, you know how the story goes—and goes. After several calls to the phone company (with no results), you write a letter, giving very specific information about the error, to the supervisor in charge of customer accounts and, finally, you get results.

Writing is also therapeutic. Talking things out on paper can help us feel better—it's a kind of free counseling session. Often, we can't express our deepest feelings to others, but we can write them. Mark Twain, in his late years, hit upon an idea that he said made him "a free man at last." That idea was "to write letters to friends & *not send them.*" His "scheme" would allow him to say what he wanted to say without offending anyone.

Writing also helps us clarify our thoughts. We can write our way to a better understanding of ourselves and of others in our lives.

Writing helps us discover things we didn't know we knew and didn't know we thought and reach new conclusions. We can solve problems as we write. Writing also helps us effectively communicate ideas when emotions interfere with speech communication. For instance, suppose your teenage daughter hasn't come home, and you are worried sick about her. You can (a.) pace the floor, wring your hands, and imagine all kinds of horrible things that could have happened to her, or (b.) you can sit down and write her a letter explaining your thoughts and feelings and telling her why you are upset. When she gets home, you can (a.) yell and scream, waking up the neighbors and driving your blood pressure to the danger zone while daughter tries desperately to ignore you and slams a few doors in defiance, or (b.) you can hand her the tear-stained letter. She will give you a quizzical look and take it to her room. When she reads it in privacy, your words will get through, and she will probably feel remorse and decide that her moments of fun were simply not worth giving you so much pain.

So, writing can help us in many ways in our daily lives—in communicating on a business or personal level. And I think everyone wants to have the ability to communicate through writing and enjoys that expression. Only in the past few years, however, have teachers begun to understand how to teach writing effectively. As a result, many people remember and dislike the feelings that the idea of writing invokes.

So, let's start over. The approach to writing in these pages will be based on the research about writing and what is called the "writing process." First, I'll tell you a little about this approach to writing. In the late 1960s, teachers such as Ken Macrorie and Peter Elbow began to talk about *freewriting*, from-the-heart writing, done at a fast pace. The idea was to practice getting words on paper—to become fluent. Concern for correctness was to come later. A few years later, researchers began to study professional writers to find out how these writers composed. Researchers discovered that these writers shared certain traits. What was learned about the habits of professional writers was developed into a schema that could be used in teaching beginning writers. Here are the stages of the writing process, but keep in mind that these stages are not always completed in a sequential order. Instead, they are recursive; writers might work back and forth within the different stages.

The process of writing

Prewriting

Think of a classroom in which an unenlightened teacher orders the class to write essays on what the students did over their summer vacations. Little Johnny gazes out the window, and the teacher walks over, raps him on the knuckles, and says, "I said, write an essay!"

Well, in fact, Little Johnny could have been doing a very important part of writing his essay: thinking about his subject. We know that professional writers may spend days or weeks or months thinking about their subjects, making notes here and there, before they actually begin to write. During this time, writers may be getting ideas for writing as they walk on the beach, drive along in their cars, or do household chores. You might be thinking, "But student writers don't have the luxury of mulling over their subjects for months before they begin writing." Actually, professionals may be driven by deadlines to speed up the thinking part of the prewriting stage. And many writers think better with a pen in hand, anyway. So, here are ways to prewrite on paper:

Focused Freewriting

Before you can write a paper, you must have ideas for that paper, and you must get them on paper. A good way to do that is to freewrite while focusing on your topic. Just start writing.

If at first the blank white paper looks intimidating, make some scribbles on it—mess it up. Remember, this is not a finished draft that you will turn in. Don't worry about correct punctuation or neatness. Don't stop to look up words you can't spell correctly. Just write—spew out your ideas and feelings about the topic. You will discover that you knew more than you thought you did. You might not use everything you have written in your final draft, but you will have started, and for many writers, getting started is the hardest part of writing.

Brainstorming

Listing or mapping is another way to get ideas on paper. Again, you might not use everything you come up with in your final paper. Write down every aspect of your topic that you can think of. You can narrow the list later, perhaps grouping some ideas together and discarding other ideas.

And brainstorming is a great way to come up with a topic in the first place. If you are given your choice of topics, you have an advantage because of the knowledge and experience you have. You may doubt my words, and you may never stop to think about exactly how you apply your taken-for-granted knowledge in the course of your studies. But trust me on this one.

I've read, I suppose, thousands of freshman essays. I have found that the experience of adult students usually comes through in more fully developed and thoughtful essays. They can draw on personal knowledge of, for instance, political issues to provide examples. When I share something— illustrate a point by way of example—with a class of young students (although I usually start out with "In the 1960s—back when dinosaurs roamed the earth"), I am proud of that knowledge, and sometimes I even feel sorry for them that they have so little before Motley Crue to serve as a frame of reference. I spend a great deal of time helping them brainstorm possible topics for the essays. They *do* know things, however, they have a reduced field of vision and some trouble relating their experience to writing.

That is not to say that adults never have problems coming up with suitable topics for writing. Adults sometimes have problems choosing from a variety of ideas; at other times, adults overlook wonderful possibilities because they take the experiences for granted. Adults, too, are less likely than those fresh out of high school to know about the reference sources available in the library (see Chapter 9). At any rate, brainstorming can help you dredge up the wonderful ideas, experiences, and feelings that make an essay exciting to read.

Outlining

Again, we're not going for a formal outline. Although some teachers still require formal outlines, most teachers believe that outlining is a tool and should not be thought of as an end in itself. Remember when I said the stages in the writing process were recursive? Many writers outline again after they have written their rough drafts to make sure their ideas hang together and that each paragraph contains support for the topic sentence.

Cubing

This technique was developed by Elizabeth Cowen. She recommends using the following headings to flesh out a topic: Describe, Compare, Associate, Analyze, Apply, and Argue.

For example, suppose you are interested in the feminist movement of the 1960s and wanted to do a paper on some aspect of the movement. You might make a list similar to the following:

Describe: The movement was political in that it advocated equal rights and equal pay for women. Leaders such as Gloria Steinem and Betty Friedan helped form a coalition that has become a powerful force in modern politics.

Associate: Bra burning became a kind of metaphor for the movement. Liberalism and a pro choice position on abortion are also associated with the movement.

Compare: The movement is similar to the women's suffrage movement and to the civil rights movement.

Analyze (look at the parts): The movement consisted of activists, who rallied and spoke at political gatherings as representatives of women, and followers who cheered the movement on and found new freedom in their personal lives. *Ms.* magazine became the first voice of the movement.

Apply: The feminist movement has resulted in real changes for American women. Although not everyone sees all the changes as positive, women now have greater freedom in whatever roles they choose. They may still vacuum the floor, but they don't do it in Harriet Nelson high heels.

Argue for or against: If you don't already have a strong position on the topic, answering questions such as the following might help you come up with a position: How do I feel about the movement? Are women better off now than they were in the 1950s? If so, in what ways? How has the movement changed over the past 25 years? What are the platforms of today's movement? With which of the stances on important issues do I agree? With which do I disagree?

There are other techniques for prewriting, but the important thing to keep in mind is this stage is for gathering ideas. Reading is also very important at this stage, and sometimes the prewriting stage may involve extensive research about your topic (see Chapter 9).

Drafting

During this stage, the writer produces what is known as a *rough draft* that may be the first of many drafts. We know that good writers often pause to re-read what they have written and write more, perhaps more than they actually will use in the final draft. Again, all stages of the writing process may be repeated as necessary. For instance, after writing a first draft, you might discover that you need more ideas for a particular section of the paper. You might brainstorm a list of possible examples or write questions that you can answer after you have done some research.

Revising

Revision might involve moving paragraphs from one position in the paper to another to achieve a more logical sequencing of ideas. Some people cut and paste to get the organization they want. Writers who work with computers might move copy blocks. During this stage, information might be added or deleted. Again, revision might be repeated with each new draft.

Editing

Editing differs from revision in that the focus is on smaller units—words, phrases, or sentences—rather than on paragraphs or large sections of the paper. Whereas organization might have been a major concern during the revision stage, the focus now is on using words and phrases effectively. For instance, the *sentence The man walked into the room* might be changed to give a better description of the action: *The tired athlete plodded into the dressing room.* During the editing stage, we also check to make sure the language we use is appropriate for the audience and check sentence structures, sometimes combining two or more sentences to eliminate wordiness. For instance, the first two sentences below might be combined to produce the third sentence:

1. Modern technology has affected humans mentally.
2. It has also affected them physically.
3. Modern technology has affected humans both mentally and physically.

Proofreading

During this stage, the writer looks for errors in punctuation, word usage, and spelling. An effective proofreading technique is to take each sentence from the bottom up, reading it aloud and checking for errors. Because we think faster than we write, it is easy to leave out words. By proofreading from the bottom up, we focus on smaller units, rather than overall meaning. Sentence fragments and run-ons become obvious as do agreement errors (see Chapter 7).

Example writing process

The following shows Debbie Rogers' writing process. Debbie had been out of high school more than ten years and had not written much, even during her high school years. She was worried about her writing abilities when she first enrolled in freshman English, but as you will see, she used the steps in the writing process to produce a fine paper. In fact, this is only one of several wonderful papers that Debbie produced during her first semester of English.

1. Debbie first wrote her opinions on a topic she cared about. (The paper was written on the second day of class. I

asked students to write their opinions about an issue they felt strongly about. I use the first writing as a general diagnostic tool to get an idea of what kinds of help students need and of their overall fluency. Although students are not expected to produce polished essays, they are encouraged to proofread and correct mechanical errors as time permits. The important thing, I stress, is to get ideas on paper. Neatness doesn't count, and they do not have to worry about a grade for the paper.

2. She pulled from the freewriting the following argument:

With every privilege comes responsibility. If you abuse the privilege, the freedom/right to exercise it may be taken from you. (Ex.: Drive car.)

This case of the NEA giving money to these artists who are producing controversial art may be an abuse of the privilege which may put the entire NEA program in jeopardy. In this instance, many artists will suffer because of the extremes of a few and the poor judgment of those given the responsibility of disbursing funds.

While Freedom of Speech is an inalicnable right, government grants are not.

3. Debbie then wrote down a purpose statement to guide her thinking and writing:

The purpose of my paper is to prove to my reader that grant money from the NEA should not be used to support art that is considered offensive and obscene.

(The first part is only to guide her as she outlines her reasons; the underlined part becomes her thesis statement.)

4. Debbie then writes down three reasons she will develop to support her thesis:

1. It is considered obscene and offensive by a majority of tax-paying citizens.
2. Refusing to fund questionable art is not the equivalent of censorship.
3. The NEA has a responsibility to exercise good judgment in the disbursement of funds and must be willing to answer to the taxpayer if it accepts public money.

(These reasons become topic sentences for sections of the paper.)

5. Since the paper required outside sources, Debbie found a newspaper story and a magazine article with information she would use to support each reason and gave credit to the source in parentheses. These sources are listed on a Works Cited page at the end of the paper.

Reasons
1. Many Americans have begun to label much of the work recently funded by the National Endowment for the Arts (NEA) as obscene and offensive. The Thomas Jefferson Center for the Protection of Free Expression recently conducted a survey in which "Three-quarters of those questioned said they favored allowing artists to display controversial works, but only one-quarter would support use of their tax dollars to pay for art displays they found offensive." (Knight-Ridder 18A)
2. Refusing to fund questionable art is not the equivalent of censorship. Rep. Richard Armey (R., Texas) said, "I'm not saying Serrano and Mapplethorpe can't produce the trash they call art. I'm just saying the American taxpayer should not be forced to pay for it."
3. The NEA has a responsibility to exercise good judgment in the disbursement of funds and must be willing to answer to the taxpayer if it accepts public funds. "The acceptance of public money implies an acceptance of a public responsibility"

(Sam Lipman, a member of the Endowment's National Council on the Arts from 1982 to 1988).

6. Debbie now is ready to write a draft, revise it for organization, etc. (many writers make several drafts before they feel it is perfected), proofread the draft, and prepare a final draft. (The following is the next to the last draft that Debbie proofed.)

[MLA Heading or Title page]

The National Endowment for the Arts (NEA) was established in 1965 to "encourage greater creativity and promote wider access to the arts." Since that time they have received $2.3 billion, with 171 million for fiscal year 1990 alone (Fitzgerald 94).

A controversy is currently brewing as many Americans have begun to label much of the work funded by the NEA as obscene. The Thomas Jefferson Center for the Protection of Free Expression, in a recently released survey, found that "Three-quarters of those questioned said they favored allowing artists to display controversial works, but only one-quarter would support use of their tax dollars to pay for art displays they found offensive" (Knight-Ridder 18 A). Andres Serrano was given $15,000 in taxpayers' money to create a picture of a crucifix submerged in a jar of his urine. This piece of art was titled "Piss Christ." The Endowment also gave $30,000 to fund a nation-wide exhibition tour of Robert Mapplethorpe's photography. Included were photos of nude children, one man urinating into another's mouth and a photograph of Mr. Mapplethorpe himself with a bullwhip protruding from his anus (Fitzgerald 93).

I believe in the minds of most Americans, this art would be judged as obscene and offensive - not something they want their tax dollars going to support.

In October 1989, Congress passed a law to prohibit federal funding for obscene works. This has been met with cries of "censorship" from many in the arts community. I believe this is a good example of the Red Herring Logical Fallacy. Those who cry censorship would like to draw the attention away from the very real complaint of the obscene and offensive nature of the art in question and would try to appeal to all people who rightfully revere our freedom of expression and try to lead them to believe that right is in danger. I personally do not believe that a refusal of funding by the NEA is the equivalent of censorship. I'm inclined to agree with Rep. Richard Armey (R., Texas), who sent the Endowment a protest letter, signed by himself and 107 colleagues saying, "I'm not saying Serrano and Mapplethorpe can't produce the trash they call art. I'm just saying the American taxpayer should not be forced to pay for it" (95). To state that refusal of funds to these artists is censorship is to say that a refusal to provide flags to protesters desiring to burn them denies their freedom of speech. If the artists are motivated by a burning desire to create this kind of work, they have the freedom to do so whether they receive federal funding or not. If it truly is a valid form of art, the art-loving segment of our society will recognize the value of it, there will be a demand for it, and it will be self-sustaining. If that does not happen, then the American public has spoken. True art shouldn't need the endorsement, promotion, or funding of the NEA to succeed or survive.

There are many legitimate forms of art that most everyone would agree are worthy and deserving of federal support. The NEA should focus it's energy and sources on this common middle-ground and stay away from controversy.

I agree with Samuel Lipman, a member of the Endowment's National Council on the Arts from 1982 to 1988: "The acceptance of public money implies an acceptance of a public responsibility. There is no argument to be made for using public funds to support trash" (95).

According to Paul Hasse, a former special assistant to the Endowment Chairman, "You're regarded as a philistine if you ask whether the public would approve of how its money is being spent on particular grants. The Endowment is extremely uncomfortable with public scrutiny" (94).

I think the NEA needs to remember where its money comes from and needs to seek harder to represent the general consensus of the American people or the very merit of the NEA's existence may be called into question. More taxpayers may decide they cannot trust the Endowment and choose to exercise their freedom of expression and speech to their lawmakers by demanding that the NEA be abolished the next time they're looking for areas to trim the "fat" out of an already strained budget. If that happens, many legitimate and deserving artists and projects will suffer due to the extremes of a few and the poor judgment of those given the responsibility of disbursing funds properly.

Works Cited [separate page]

Fitzgerald, Randy. "Our Tax Dollars for This Kind of Art?" The Reader's Digest Apr. 1990: 93-96.

Knight-Ridder Newspapers. "Free-Speech Survey Shows Conflicts." The Dallas Morning News 15 Sept. 1990: 18A.

As you can see, Debbie put herself into this essay. Research tells us that people write best about topics they really care about, and it is clear that Debbie has strong feelings about the NEA controversy. Some instructors would require that Debbie use fewer first-person pronouns for such an essay, citing the following reasons:

1. In an argumentative essay, the opinions expressed are automatically taken to be those of the writer unless stated otherwise.
2. Simply stating an opinion, without the ""I think . . ."" makes a more forceful argument. (Example: "I personally do not believe that a refusal of funding by the NEA is the

equivalent of censorship" is stronger as "A refusal of funding by the NEA is not the equivalent of censorship."

Of course, assertions should be supported with good reasons, facts, examples, etc. Debbie supports her assertion with a quotation from a congressman and with an analogy (comparison to the flag-burning issue). And sometimes it is necessary for a writer to clarify that the opinion she is asserting is her own and not that of, perhaps, someone else she has just quoted.

Note: Don't throw away your final papers or give them to people without making a copy. One of my students wrote a wonderful paper about how women were used in advertising to portray certain images. She was proud of it and sent it to her sister to read. When she asked her sister about it later, the sister said she thought she threw it away. Remember the earlier advice about making a copy before you hand in a paper to an instructor. The same goes for giving your last copy to someone else.

Using writing samples

A way to learn indirectly about writing is to read the writing of others. When you are assigned to write a type of paper that you have not written before, look for samples of that kind of writing. Professional writers, like students, read the work of others before they begin to write a new kind of writing. For instance, a writer who wants to write a book review for *Harper's* would first look up some back issues of the magazine and study the style and format of the book reviews. Before a novelist writes his first novel, he or she reads many other novels. Before a person writes a letter to the editor of the local newspaper, he or she is likely to read other letters to find out what characteristics those letters have in common.

Here are some questions to ask when studying sample writing:

1. What is the writer's purpose for writing the piece?
2. To whom does the writer seem to be speaking?
3. How does the writer develop ideas? With details? With examples? With statistics?
4. How does the writer organize the information or details in the piece? In chronological (time) order? In order of most to least important? In spatial order? By categories?
5. What transitions does the writer use to make the writing smooth and easy-to-follow?
6. What is the writer's tone, or attitude toward the subject?
7. What do you notice about the length and kind of sentences?
8. Does the author use words that are only understood by people in certain vocations or professions?
9. If the piece is persuasive, what kinds of support does the writer use?

Taking essay exams

When researchers compared the writing of students who failed and those who passed the writing portion of entry exams, they discovered certain characteristics of both. The failing papers were usually "lean," or shorter, than the passing papers. One researcher found that the tendency to write lean papers was also found in the adult work world. What we might glean from this is that adults have learned short cuts of communication. They use expressions that say a lot. For instance, in a commercial for *Inc.* magazine, a woman executive says, "I don't have time to re-invent the wheel."

Instead of a lengthy explanation that trying things that have been tried by others and failed or neglecting the good ideas of others that have been proven to work can take time away from activities that lead to success, she used an expression that quickly communicates an idea.

Although the papers of young writers may be lean for other reasons (lack of development or support of an idea), the bottom line is that lean papers fail on standardized tests. The same logic may be present in both failing and passing papers; however, it is often less obvious in failing papers. The passing papers, or "stout" papers, usually have an obvious organization. Although they may be padded (have unnecessary words and repetitions), they show a clear development of idea and support.

You have just read about the writing process and can see that producing a polished paper can be a lengthy process. Yet, when you take a writing test, you have a limited amount of time—not to mention the fact that you are writing under high-stress conditions.

Here are some of the possible prompts for essay exams that are given for placement purposes:

The prompt will probably be a brief scenerio, or situation. You might be asked to write a paper in which you, for instance, persuade a newspaper audience that your town should or should not build a new football stadium.

You will usually be given some idea of who the audience is for the paper. Now, you know that the *real* audience for the paper is the teacher who will grade the paper. But you must play the game and pretend to be writing to the audience specified in the prompt. You also know that the real purpose of writing the paper is to pass the test, but you are expected to play the game and assume the specified purpose.

Of the things looked for by the graders of essay exams, organization and how well the writer addressed the purpose and audience specified in the prompt are very important.

Survival tip: Essay exams

Here are some tricks to get you through:

1. Get comfortable (take your shoes off; loosen your belt), breath deeply, and think of the exam as a chance to show off how much you have learned about writing.

2. Read the prompt through once to get a general idea of what is expected.

3. Read the prompt a second time, looking for key words such as *define, explain, persuade*, etc.

4. Write on a scrap piece of paper this sentence starter: The purpose of my paper is to prove to my audience that _____. (What follows the word "that" can usually serve as a thesis, or main idea, for the paper, especially if the paper is a persuasive paper.) You don't need the sentence starter in your paper.

5. Write the word *Audience* on your scrap paper to remind yourself of the (fake) audience. Example: Audience— school board members

6. Brainstorm a list of reasons or supporting details.

7. Arrange the ideas in a logical sequence.

8. Write an introduction that includes the main idea of your essay.

9. Write a paragraph or several paragraphs, depending on the required length of the assignment, about each aspect of your topic.

10. Write a conclusion that summarizes the main point of your essay (not in the same words you used in the introduction) and gives your reader a sense of completeness (as opposed to the idea that you ran out of paper or reached 300 words and quit).

11. Read over what you have written. Look for unsupported opinions or ideas. (Example: *The citizens already have high taxes.*)

12. Draw lines to the back of the paper and write examples or additional information to support the opinions or ideas (Example: *For instance, just last year, taxpayers passed a bond issue that required a 3 percent jump in school taxes. Although the townspeople have been supportive of the school system, there is a limit to what many families can afford. Since the cost of living has increased more than household income in the past few years, many families are already having to cut back on purchases of both luxury and necessary items.*)

13. Recopy the paper, inserting the sentences you have written on the back of the paper.

14. Proofread the final paper, neatly making necessary corrections.

Additional tips:

If the writing prompt asks for an essay of 300 to 500 words, you can be sure that an essay of 150 words will not pass. Find out how many words you average per page in your normal handwriting. It is not necessary to count words, but you want to be safely within the required word count. That may mean writing out a page and counting words beforehand to get an average word-per-page count.

Remember, you are writing in a simulated situation. In other words, you are not bound to tell the truth and nothing but the truth. Suppose you were asked to compare life in the dorm with life at home. What if you have never lived in a dorm and can only imagine what it must be like? That's exactly what you must do—imagine, fabricate. It's not really lying, and you will not be shot at sunrise. I know students who have failed essay exams because the prompt didn't apply to them. They wasted their time trying to force the prompt to relate to them personally. Test developers now try to choose prompts that relate to a general population, but there is still the possibility that you will get a bad prompt. If that happens, go into fairy-tale mode. Make up examples, anecdotes, whatever is necessary.

Chapter 9

The Research Process

You will probably be asked to write a number of research papers during your college career. Although research papers are not necessarily the same as term papers, many term papers involve library research. Some may involve different kinds of research—perhaps laboratory research, surveying attitudes and opinions through questionnaires, or closely observing the behaviors of a selected group of people. Some assignments will require only a limited number of resources; others will require a thorough search through the existing sources about your topic. Other papers may involve analysis and/or evaluation of a work of literature. But here we will talk about the method of collecting and reporting information for a library research paper, keeping in mind that once you have learned the research process in general, you can use it to do other kinds of research—perhaps for an oral presentation or debate.

The Research Paper:
Torture test or learning tool?

At first it may be hard to see the value in doing a research paper. Your time is already stretched from here to there, and you certainly don't have time for busy work. Research papers involve not only hours in the library but also dotting *i*'s and crossing *t*'s on the final draft—making sure that all documentation conforms to a specific style, and that may include using a space instead of a comma or putting a period here and not there in your Works Cited sheet. In fact, the whole thing may seem to be a lot of nit-picking.

I had the same feeling when I was forced to take Plane Geometry in high school. I did not plan to spend my life looking at circles and squares and angles. I thought it was extremely short-sighted of the school to make the course a requirement for graduation. Why couldn't I take something that would be useful? It was only after resignation to the fact that I couldn't get out of taking the course that I actually began to enjoy it a little. It was years later that I realized that Plane Geometry wasn't about circles and squares and angles—it was about thinking.

And so it is with the research paper. The object is not to make you run around in circles and sweat over whether you should put a period, a comma, or nothing at a particular place in your bibliography and spend hours backtracking because you forgot to write down a page number. The object is to help you develop skills you will use throughout your college career and in your chosen profession. You will examine the aspects of a particular topic and search out details. You will investigate the topic, using the resources of the library— resources you may not have known existed. You will use higher-order thinking skills in organizing and synthesizing the information into a paper. You will pay attention to detail in preparing your final draft and bibliography. In fact, you will have a chance to show off your determination to do well in college. You will explore new ideas and contribute to the body of knowledge about a specific topic.

Although you might not publish your contribution, you will have learned. Ideally, you will share this knowledge with your classmates, or at least with a partner who reads your paper to help with revision and editing. And for those students who do not do their best on exams because of the time pressures, the research paper offers them a chance to shine. They will have time to prepare a really fine representation of what they have learned.

The literary research paper

In the past, the literary research paper was a standard part of freshman English curricula. Instructors threw out these assignments and expected their students to know how to write them. Students, confused as hell—even if they had written some kind of research paper in high school—turned in papers that were composed of "patchwork plagiarism." Because they didn't really understand the literary criticism (articles in English journals) they read and felt insecure about incorporating the information they found into their papers, they took ideas from the articles they read and tried to weave them into a paper. Instructors often slashed these papers to ribbons and wondered why their students were so dumb.

The problem was that literary criticism is written on an intentionally high level. It is full of jargon and complex sentence structures. It is written to a very specific audience— English professors. Only people who have studied the *language* of the literary world, who understand the words used in literary criticism, can read literary criticism with full understanding. People who can understand literary criticism constitute, maybe, five percent of the population; people who *want* to understand literary criticism number far fewer.

Today, enlightened instructors do not require literary research papers of lower level students, at least, not without very precise instructions and guidance. I enjoy doing literary research papers, but I know that not everyone does. As far as non-English majors are concerned, literary research papers should be reserved as punishment for axe murderers.

If you plan to major in English, you should certainly expect to master the literary research paper in upper level courses. If you do not and are assigned such a paper in a lower-level English course, my advice is to set up regular appointments with your teacher and get guidance with each step.

If you are not assigned a specific topic, you will produce a better paper if you choose a topic that interests you. Even if you are assigned to write about a certain event or work of literature, you can choose an aspect of that event or work that is related to something you know about.

Suppose, for instance, you were assigned to write a paper on the *Adventures of Huckleberry Finn*. Perhaps you're not really into Twain's use of the river as a symbol in the novel— maybe you don't really understand it. Perhaps you don't feel competent to piece together literary criticism. But, let's say you are interested in the topic of censorship. You might research when and why the novel has been banned, from the time of its release to the present. You would, however, want to have any topic approved by your instructor.

Topic selection for a research paper

You will probably be given at least a general idea of what the research paper should be about. For a history class, for instance, you will know what period and what aspects of that period have been focused on in the course. The instructor will probably give even more specific instructions. For instance, she may ask that you do a paper on World War II. Well, many books have been written about World War II. In fact, you couldn't begin to cover the topic in anything less than a book. You can, however, deal with a very limited aspect of the war in a research paper. So you begin by asking yourself some questions:

1. What aspect of the war really caught my interest when I was reading?
2. Did my instructor say something that made me want to know more about what he mentioned?
3. What are some of my interests in general?
4. How does something I am interested in relate to World War II?

Suppose, for instance, you are interested in the change in women's rights and roles. You might ask yourself the following questions:

- What was the average American woman like before World War II?
- What was her role in the home?
- What was her role in society?
- What did women do at home during the war?
- How many women served in the war?
- What did they do?

Suppose you become interested in the role of women in the war and want to know whether women served in roles other than nursing. As you are looking through some general sources, you find a reference to the women pilots of World War II. Ah, ha! You didn't know that women served as pilots, and you want to know more about those female pilots. You start digging and find that about 1,000 women served as pilots during the war. Since women did not fly combat missions, you want to know exactly what they did. So you're off. You want some answers to your questions. You might run across some names and look for personal accounts written by one or more of these women. As you search, you formulate new questions and look for new answers and decide on a specific angle of attack for your paper.

Library sources

In review of the resources in the library, the following list includes resources that you are likely to use during your research. If you live some distance from a large university library, you can use the local library. Even smaller libraries usually have an inter-loan service through which they can borrow books and copies of articles from other libraries.

Note: Most libraries have scheduled tours through which students are introduced to the various resources and their locations. You will probably want to get in on one of these early in your school career.

Card Catalog

A card catalog is a file that contains cards for each book in a library. In fact, there are usually three cards for each book, with one filed in each of the three divisions of the card catalog. One will be filed under the author's name. The Name section of the card catalog contains names of the authors of books and usually names of people books are written about. To find a book in this section, you must know the author's last name (unless you are researching a particular person—e.g. Thomas Jefferson).

In the Title section of the card catalog, books are filed by specific titles. The alphabetical arrangement disregards first words such as *the* and *a*. To find a book titled *The Language of the Heart*, you would look in the *L* section instead of the *T* section.

Books in the Subject section are filed by general topic and subtopic. For instance, if you are looking for a book about modern music, you would first go to the Music section, then look for the History and Criticism section, then go on until you find the 20th Century section.

Each card contains a call number in the upper left-hand corner. The call number is the filing number. For instance, a book by or about Mark Twain would have a PE13— call number in a library that uses the Library of Congress filing system. You would go to the PE section to find the book. In a small library that uses the Dewey system, the call number would start with 810, the number class for American literature. It is not necessary to know the number for the different classifications. Larger libraries have charts that will tell you the floor and section that houses the different classifications. In small libraries, the books should be arranged in a logical order that allows you to follow the numbers from one section to the next. The aisles will be labeled with starting and ending numbers.

A word about computers

Now that you know how to use the card catalog, I'll tell you that no one uses the files much. Now people sit down at a computer terminal in the library and type in a few words to find the call number of a book. The numbers are still the same; the information is just easier to find.

As with the card catalog, you can use the print version or the on-line version. The on-line version is faster and easier to use. If you have not spent much time with computers, the library is a good place to get experience. Someone will help you get started, and the rest is easy. Adults tend to fear computers at first. Actually, they fear doing something stupid and blowing up the thing. If you fear blowing up a computer—don't. There is nothing you will do to a computer that can't be undone. And the programs are so "user friendly" now that they seem to lead humans by the hand. Try doing a search for articles on a subject that interests you. You will wonder why you waited so long. And don't be embarrassed about asking young students to help. Computers are their domain; they love to teach adults and are usually very patient.

General Indexes

The card catalog only contains books. For journal articles or articles in magazines, you will need to look up your subject in an index. For papers on general topics, you can go to the *Reader's Guide*; for papers in specific fields, you may need to look for articles in any one of a number of indexes.

Reader's Guide to Periodical Literature

The *Reader's Guide* lists articles that are published in magazines that are read by the general public. An article in a magazine like *Psychology Today* is listed in the *Reader's Guide*, but an article in a journal like the *Journal of American Psychology* would be listed in the *Social Sciences Index*. An article about Thomas Jefferson might be found in a magazine such as *American Heritage*, listed in the *Reader's Guide*, but a scholarly article about his work will be found in *The MLA* (Modern Language Association) *Bibliography*.

Special Indexes

There are indexes that cover any field you choose to major in. The following is a sample list of the many indexes: *Agriculture Index, Index to Speeches, The Education Index, Engineering Index*. The list goes on. You should be familiar with the index that contains information on articles in your field. During your first two years of college, you might get by with using only the *Reader's Guide* and the card catalog to find sources, but as you get into courses in your major field, you will be asked to do more involved research.

Once you find a promising-looking article in a general or specific index, you then must find the article itself. Libraries have lists of their journals and magazines. Look for this list and see whether the periodical you want is available in the library. If not, you are faced with ordering the article through inter-loan or using another article.

In addition to the books and journals, libraries have all kinds of general reference sources. If you want information on a contemporary author, you can look in the *Contemporary Author* series; if you want to know how many people were enrolled in college in 1990, you can look in an almanac; if you want to know who Lee Iococca is, you can look in *Who's Who in America*. The number of sources is unimaginable. Whatever you want to know, you can find in a large library. And when you aren't sure where to start looking, just ask a librarian. Librarians are in the business of knowing where to look, and knowing where to look is part of their work. You will probably find that your librarian is not only willing but also eager to help.

Note: Library research takes much time and patience. It's not a good idea to leave the kids in the car with the windows rolled up when you go into the library for even just *one little article*.

Making a working bibliography

As you begin your research, make a working bibliography. Some people use a separate 3x5 card for each book or article; some people use plain paper and list the books, writing only on one side for handling ease later on. The card or sheet contains the call number of the book, the author's name, the title, and the publishing information (place, publisher, and date). For articles, include the author, article title, magazine or journal title, volume number, page numbers, and publication date. If you are using different libraries, you might also want to include the location of the book. After you find the book and scan it for the kind of information you need, you might note on the card how useful the source might be.

Making sure you get down all the relevant information is important because you will need it when you prepare your bibliography. However, when you start collecting your information, you might want to make copies of sections of books that you can use. If you do this, make sure you note the source on the copies. I learned this the hard way by making copies of pages in books and later not knowing which book the pages came from. Of course, at the time I was sure that I would remember, but sleeping does things to my memory. After some time-consuming back-tracking, I learned to write down the information on the copies or to copy the title and copyright pages of the book and paper clip them to the copied section.

For journal articles, you will have to sit in the library to read them and make notes or copy the article. Again, if you copy the article, write down the bibliographic information.

Making notes from sources

When you begin reading your sources, you can translate the author's words into your own as you go or wait until later to translate the information. Many people prefer to use note cards for all notes so that they can arrange them according to topic. Other people use highlighters on sections of the copies they want to use in their papers and number the sections according to topic. If you are using note cards, remember to put page numbers for the information and quotation marks around anything that you have taken word-for-word from the source. Any direct quotation must be exact, so double-check what you have written against the original. Again, you might think you will remember later which notes are direct quotations, but chances are you won't. There are too many other things to remember. If you make your notes thorough, you won't have to rely on memory. Thorough notes pay off when it comes time to actually write the paper.

Important Note: Keeping your notes together, whether in a banded stack of note cards or in a spiral notebook, will pay off, too. I am likely to grab any available scrap of paper and hurriedly scribble barely legible notes, but I have paid dearly for this bad habit. Periodically, I have to collect all the scraps of paper, try to decipher them, and file them so that I can use them when I need them. I have spent hours looking for a particular note or quotation. Developing good habits at this early stage will help you now and later.

Pulling your information together

Making a good outline will help you organize your reading and your writing. Don't worry about how formal the outline looks. The numbers and letters don't have to line up exactly. The outline is for you unless your instructor wants a formal outline. Start by listing the aspects of your topic. (See Debbie Rogers' sample in Chapter 8). Next, do some brainstorming and group the ideas into a logical arrangement. Then, make an outline, arranging the subtopics in logical order (time order, order of importance, etc.).

Keying your notes into your outline is a good idea. You can do this with numbers or letters. The important thing is that, when you begin writing, you can go right to the appropriate note card or passage in your copied pages.

Incorporating sources into your paper

The following was adapted from an exercise written by Edith Wynne, professor at Texas A & M University-Commerce. It is an effective way to learn the different ways to incorporate someone else's words into your own writing.

SUMMARIZING, PARAPHRASING, AND QUOTING

Key terms

Summary: A condensed report of the main ideas.

Paraphrase: A rewording that preserves the meaning of something spoken or written.

Quotation: Repeated, using the same words as the original. Credit is given to the original source.

Ellipsis: Series of three periods used to indicate that words or sentences have been omitted.

ORIGINAL PASSAGE FROM THE SOURCE:

Gravity and its pulling force on an object gives the object weight. The weight of an object is proportional to its mass, or the amount of matter in the object. The weight of an object will change as it travels further away from the earth's surface, but its mass will remain constant. (Technical, *Elements of Mechanics* 14)

SUMMARY

The weight of an object depends on its mass and its closeness to the earth's surface. Although an object's mass, or amount of matter, does not change, the object's weight varies because of the pull of gravity as the object comes closer to the earth (Technical 14).

PARAPHRASE

The force of gravity on objects gives them weight. The weight of objects is related to mass, or quantity of matter contained in objects. As objects move away from the earth's surface, their weight changes; however, mass does not change (Technical 14).

DIRECT QUOTATION

"The weight of an object will change as it travels further away from the earth's surface, but its mass will remain constant" (Technical 14).

PARAPHRASE WITH QUOTED MATERIAL

The force of gravity on an object gives it weight, which "is proportional to its mass, or the amount of matter in the object" (Technical 14).

QUOTATION WITH ELLIPSIS

"Gravity and its pulling force on an object give the object weight [which] is proportional to its mass, or the amount of matter in the object. . . . [I]ts mass will remain constant" (Technical 14).

PRACTICE 1

1. What is the difference in the length of the summary and that of the original source?

   _____

2. In the summary, is the word or sentence order changed from the original source?

   _____

3. What is the value of summarizing?

   _____

4. In the paraphrase, is the word or sentence order changed from the original source?

_____

5. How is a paraphrase different from a summary?

_____

6. Why would you need to paraphrase?

_____

7. How is the direct quotation different from the original?

_____

8. For what reasons might you use a direct quotation?

_____

9. Why might you want to use a combination of paraphrased and quoted material?

_____

10. What does the ellipsis indicate?

_____

PRACTICE 2

Write a summary, paraphrase, and paraphrase with quoted material based on the following original passage:

ORIGINAL PASSAGE

Newton's first law of motion is stated as follows: A body at rest will remain at rest, and a body in motion will continue in motion with undiminished speed in a straight line, as long as no unbalanced external force acts upon it. (Technical, *Elements of Mechanics* 23)

Note: Quotations of four or more lines are indented ten spaces from the left margin. The ending period comes before the parenthetical citation. For shorter quotations that are incorporated into the text, the period comes after the parentheses.

SUMMARY

_____
_____
_____
_____

PARAPHRASE

_____
_____
_____
_____

PARAPHRASE WITH QUOTED MATERIAL

_____
_____
_____
_____
_____

Using outside sources

Reasons to Include Outside Sources
1. To use experts to lend credibility to your report or proposal
2. To use data or specific facts to support your main point
3. To let people speak for themselves, avoiding misunderstandings that can result from inaccurate translations

Reasons to Document Sources
1. To give credit where credit is due. Not giving credit amounts to plagiarism, stealing another's words or ideas.

2. To give your reader the information he needs to find the original source so he may read further.

Ways to incorporate published sources

Including Source Information in Text
Short reports or proposals with few sources usually have relevant source information included in the text.
Example:
In *Agents of Influence* (Touchstone, 1990), Pat Choate notes that "Japanese firms can invest and sell in America, but American firms find it difficult to invest and sell in Japan."

Parenthetical Citations and Works Cited Lists
The name of the author may be enclosed in parentheses, along with the page number where the quotation may be found, at the end of the quoted material. If more than one work by the same author is listed on the Works Cited page, a short form of the title should be included with each parenthetical citation.

Works Cited pages contain all of the sources referred to listed in alphabetical order. The Modern Language Association style is used most often. Books are listed with the following information: author (last name, first name), title (underlined or italicized), place of publication, publisher, year of publication. Newspaper and magazine articles contain the title of the article and the page numbers.
Example:
Ambrose, Stephen E. *The Victors: Eisenhower and His Boys: The Men of World War II*. New York: Simon & Schuster, 1998.

Collins, Glenn. "Single-Father Survey Finds Adjustment a
Problem." *New York Times* 21 Nov. 1983: B17.

Note: Remember that using as few as three words, words
that have a special meaning as they are put together without
giving credit to the original author can be plagiarism. Make
sure that you have given credit for the ideas as well as any
directly quoted material. Documentation is the way we give
credit in writing.

Documentation styles

Although there are several different styles of
documentation, the two most popular ones both use
parenthetical documentation instead of footnotes. Yes, things
have changed since you were in high school, and the whole
process is easier now. You no longer have to re-type to line up
footnotes. Any footnotes you might use in addition to
parenthetical documentation can be quickly inserted with a
word processing program.

In English classes, you will probably be asked to use
MLA (Modern Language Association) style. In psychology
classes, you will probably be asked to use APA (American
Psychological Association) style. In other classes, you might
be able to choose the style and use the one with which you are
most familiar or with which you need to become familiar. If
you plan to major in the social sciences, for instance, you will
probably want to use APA style when you are given a choice.
The important thing is that you do use some style sheet
(actually in a book) and maintain consistency. Many textbooks
now include examples of documentation style, and the MLA
Style Manual and APA *Publication Manual* are available at
college bookstores.

Manuscript form

When you write or type your final paper, be sure to leave margins all the way around and number mark each page with your last name and the page number. You may be required to attach a cover sheet in a specific format and to bind the paper in a certain way. Some instructors prefer the pages be paper clipped together. Others might want the paper submitted in a folder. Although you can buy report covers, clear plastic covers with a spine binder, I haven't met a teacher who likes the things. They are just in the way during the grading process, and the little spine binder is likely to fly off as the instructor turns the pages.

Survival Tip: Savor the feeling

After you have finished your paper, you can sit back and enjoy the feeling of accomplishment. You have gone through the same process that a writer goes through to write a book. The process will get easier each time you do it, and you will feel confident as you approach your next research project.

Chapter 10
Quick Math Review

The following math review was prepared by Judy Taylor, who teaches both high school and beginning college math. If you have trouble with this quiz, you will probably want to take a noncredit developmental course before you begin your regular math courses. As I noted before, math courses can be both difficult and time-consuming for those who have forgotten much of their high school math. The idea is to be prepared to succeed in college math. That may mean taking noncredit courses or using the campus math lab to brush-up with a tutor or on a computer. On the other hand, if you breeze right through the quiz below, you may be ready for college math. You may want to check out a basic math text at the library before you take a placement exam at college.

QUIZ

1. Mr. Smith bought $3.78 worth of ground meat, a head of lettuce for $.69, $1.29 worth of tomatoes, and a jar of pickles for $1.89. How much change did he get if he paid for these items with a ten dollar bill?

2. What will a teacher's aide working six hours and twenty minutes earn if her rate of pay is six dollars and thirty cents per hour?

3. Four cups of a floor cleaner is to be mixed with twelve gallons of water. To clean a small school, it will take

five gallons of cleaner. How much water will be needed to dilute that much cleaner?

4. A discount store sells everything at fifty percent off the list price. During an after-Christmas sale, the store took an additional one-fourth off. If the list price for a dress is eighty dollars, what would the dress cost during the sale?

5. On a map, a distance of ten feet is represented by one inch. How long must a line be to represent a distance of 250 feet?

6. The speed limit on most highways is 55 miles per hour. How far will a car travel in ten hours?

7. Peggy purchased a $2,000 piano. She made a down payment of $250 and agreed to pay a 1 1/2% finance charge per month on any unpaid balance. How much did she owe at the end of the first month?

8. What is the diameter of the largest ball that will fit in a square with a side measurement of 19 inches?

9. A playground is 30 by 40 feet. How much shorter is it to cross the playground diagonally than to walk around the two sides?

10. Let y stand for Yolanda's age. Her mother is 3 more than 9 times Yolanda's age. Write this as an algebraic expression.

11. Solve $(6x2 - 2x) - (2x2 + 2x)$

12. Find the sum: $(+3) + (-7) + (+2) + (-3)$

13. Find the difference: $(-4) - (-3) - (+2)$

14. Solve for the variable: $3x = 15$

ANSWERS AND EXPLANATIONS

1. The first step is to add his four purchases. The second step is to subtract the total from $10.

STEP 1:	$3.78	STEP 2:	$10.00
	.69		- 7.64
	1.28		2.36
	1.89		
	$7.64		

With problems that are similar to this, be careful to make sure that you are answering the question that is asked. It would be very easy to stop after adding the items, but you will notice that the amount of change left out of a ten dollar bill is asked for. Therefore, you must subtract the total from ten to get the answer to this problem.

2. Answer: $39.90. For this problem, several steps must be included to come up with a final answer. Think about what you know. You know the teacher's aide makes $6.30 per hour and has worked a little over 6 hours. There are several ways you can work this problem.

(a)　First you must determine what fractional part of an hour 20 minutes is. With 60 minutes in an hour, what part of the whole is 20 minutes?
　　　　　20/60 or 1/3
　　　Therefore, she has worked 6 1/3 hours. For every hour she works, she makes $6.30. Multiply $6.30 times 6 1/3, and you have an answer of $39.90.

(b)　Making tables is another way to solve problems:

Table 2A

HOURS WORKED	TOTAL PAYMENT
1	$ 6.30
2	$12.60
3	$18.90
4	$25.20
5	$31.50
6	$37.80
7	$44.10

Table 2B

PARTIAL HOURS	AMOUNT PAID
10 min. = 1/6	$1.05
20 min. = 1/3	$2.10
30 min. = 1/2	$3.15
40 min. = 2/3	$4.20
50 min. = 5/6	$5.25

From Table 2A, take the amount she was paid for 6 hours of work ($27.80). Then from Table 2B, take the amount for 20 minutes ($2.10). Add the two amounts ($39.90).

(c)   Another way to work this problem is to change the time to a decimal and multiply by 6.30.

3.   Answer: 240 gallons. This problem can be solved using ratio and proportions.

$$\frac{4 \text{ cups of cleaner}}{12 \text{ gallons of water}} = \frac{5 \text{ gallons of cleaner}}{x \quad \text{gallons of water}}$$

This set up is a proportion, but there is one small problem. The unit of measurement must be the same. Four cups of cleaner cannot equal to 5 gallons of cleaner. You must change 5 gallons to cups. To do that, you must know how many cups are in one gallon. If that's not something you can instantly recall, use what you do know to find the answer. For instance, you probably know that there are 2 cups in a pint and 2 pints in a quart and 4 quarts in a gallon. So, there you have it: 16 cups in a gallon. In this problem there are 5 gallons of cleaner; so multiply 16 times 5 to get how many cups in 5 gallons (80 cups).

$$\frac{4}{1} = \frac{80}{x} \qquad \frac{4}{12} \qquad \frac{80}{x} \qquad \begin{array}{l} 4x = 12(80) \\ 4x = \quad 960 \end{array}$$

To solve this, you must then cross multiply (12 x 80=960 and 4x). The result is divided by 4. Therefore, x = 240.

4.   Answer: $30. First, take 50% of 80. You can do this one of two ways. You can take 1/2 of 80 or multiply 80 times .50 and get $40.00. Here again, you are not finished with the problem. It asks for the price of the

garment after the Christmas sale (an additional 1/4 off). You can either take 1/4 of 40 or multiply 40 times .25 and get $10. The $10 is the amount of the 25% discount; therefore, you must subtract $10 from $40 to get the price of the garment ($30.00).

5. Answer: 25 inches. A proportion may be used here.

$$\frac{1 \text{ inch}}{10 \text{ feet}} = \frac{x \text{ inches}}{250 \text{ feet}}$$

Cross multiply to obtain $10x = 250$

$$x = 25$$

6. Answer: 550 miles. Multiply 55 mph times 10 hours to obtain 550 miles. You may also use a proportion to set this up. If you learn how to use ratio and proportions, you can solve just about any problem.

$$\frac{55 \text{ miles}}{1 \text{ hour}} = \frac{x}{10x \text{ hours}}$$

$$x = 550 \text{ miles}$$

7. Answer 1776.25. First, subtract $250 from $2,000 and get $1750. Then multiply .015 times 1750 (26.25) and add 26.25 to 1750 to get 1776.25

8. Answer: 19 inches. When you are dealing with stated problems, drawing a sketch or picture can be very helpful. The problem asks for the largest ball that can fit in a square with sides 19 inches long.

19 inches

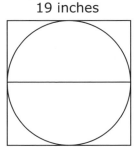

From the sketch, you can readily see that the largest ball that can be placed inside the square will have a diameter of 19 inches.

9. Answer: 20 feet. Use the Pythagorean theorem (see explanation later in chapter) to find the length of the diagonal path. A sketch is very important here.

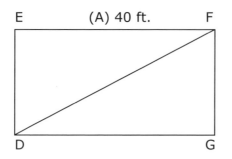

The walk from corner D to corner E and then on to corner F = 70 feet. To walk directly from D to F is only 50 feet. The diagonal path is 20 feet shorter.

10. Answer: $9y + 3$

Add 3 to 9 times y. Therefore, $9y + 3$ represents this statement.

11. Answer: $4x^2 - 4x$. This problem is a subtraction algebra problem. When a subtraction sign is in front of parentheses, it means to change all the signs inside the parentheses: $(6x^2 - 2x) - (2x^2 + 2x)$ becomes $6x - 2x - 2x^2 - 2x$. Then collect like terms. Remember x^2 and x are not common factors. They cannot be added or subtracted, but you can add $6x^2 - 2x^2$ and get $4x^2$, then $-2x - 2x = -4x$. So, $(6x^2 - 2x) - (2x^2 + 2x) = 4x^2 - 4x$.

12. Answer: -5. The rules for adding integers (positive and negative numbers) are (1.) Like signs add and take that sign. (Example: $2 + 3 = 5$ or $-2 + -3 = -5$) and (2.) When you subtract unlike signs, take the sign of the larger number. (Ex: $-7 + 8 = +1$; $7 + -11 = -4$)

13. Answer: -3. The rule for subtracting integers is (1.) Change the sign of the second number and use the rules for addition. Therefore, every subtraction problem becomes an addition problem. $(-4) - (-3) - (+2)$ becomes $(-4) + (+3) + (-2) = -3$.

14. Answer: $x = 5$. First of all, a variable is a letter (*a, b, c, x, y, z*, etc.) that takes the place of a number. When solving for a variable, you are trying to find what number the variable is replacing. Find what operation (+, −, ×, ÷) is taking place, then do the opposite. In problem 14, $3x$ means 3 is being multiplied by the variable. The opposite of multiplying is dividing, so divide both sides of the equation by 3.

$$\frac{3x}{3} = \frac{15}{3}$$

Three will go into 3 one time; 15 divided by 3 equals five; therefore, $x = 5$. Check by replacing the *x* with 5 in the equation.

A brief review

DECIMALS

1. When adding or subtracting decimals, remember to keep the decimal straight. For example, .04 + 1.89 = 1.93.

$$\begin{array}{r} .04 \\ +\ 1.89 \\ \hline 1.93 \end{array}$$

2. When multiplying decimals, multiply as if the decimal was not there and then count the number of decimals and mark them off from right to left. For example:

$$2.5 \times .3 = \begin{array}{r} 2.5 \\ \times\ .3 \\ \hline 75 \end{array} = .75$$

3. When dividing decimals, you must first move the decimal in the divisor to make a whole number and move the decimal in the dividend the same number of times you moved it in the divisor. (32.8 divided by .4 = 82).

FRACTIONS

1. When adding or subtracting fractions, you must have a common denominator—the bottom number of a fraction must be the same to add or subtract them. For example: 4/5 + 3/5 = 7/5, but 1/2 + 1/3 = ?, so you

must find a common denominator before adding or subtracting (6 because 2 and 3 will go into it an even number of times).

$$1/2 = 3/6$$
$$1/3 = 2/6$$

The fractions can now be added or subtracted.

2. When multiplying fractions, you must multiply the numerator times the numerator and the denominator times the denominator. For example: $2/7 \times 4/5 = 8/35$

3. To divide fractions, just invert and multiply. For example: To divide 3/5 by 2/7, first invert 2/7 to 7/2 and then multiply

$$3/5 \div 2/7 = ?$$
$$3/5 \times 7/2 = 21/10$$

PERCENTS

When dealing with percents, you must first change that percent to a decimal by moving the decimal two places to the left. (Example: 25% of 48 = .25 × 48 = 12)

If you are asked to write a percent as a fraction in lowest terms, you simply take your percent and put it over 100 and reduce it. (25% as a fraction is 25/100 = 1/4)

RATIOS AND PROPORTIONS

Ratios and proportions are important concepts to learn and understand. Many problems can be solved using ratios and proportions. A ratio is another name for *fraction*. It can be written 1/4 or 1:4 (1 is to 4). A proportion is two equivalent ratios: 1/4 = 2/8. To test whether two ratios are proportional, cross multiply, and if they are equal, the ratios are proportional. With 1 × 8 = 8 and 2 × 4 = 8, the ratios are equal and proportional. Quiz problem number 3 can be solved by using proportion. When using proportion, you must remember to keep your units of measure equal.

$$\frac{4 \text{ cups of cleaner}}{12 \text{ gallons of water}} = \frac{80 \text{ cups of cleaner}}{\text{x gallons of water}}$$

or

$$\frac{4 \text{ cups of cleaner}}{80 \text{ gallons of water}} = \frac{12 \text{ cups of cleaner}}{\text{x gallons of water}}$$

In each case, cups of cleaner is paired with gallons of water, either across from each other or in a ratio.

When you cross multiply in either problem, you will get the following: $4x = 960$ and $x = 240$.

PYTHAGOREAN THEOREM

This theorem deals with a right triangle and states that if you square one side and add it to the square of the other side, it is equal to the square of the hypotenuse. The following diagram may be of some help.

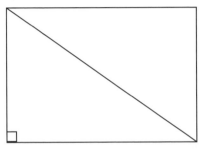

If $a = 3$ and $b = 4$, then $c = 5$ because 3 squared = 9 and 4 squared = 16. When you add them together, you get 25. The problem will then be c squared = 25; therefore $c = 5$.

$$9 + 16 = c^2$$
$$25 = c^2$$
$$c = 5$$

POST QUIZ

1. Mr. Jones bought $7.78 worth of ground meat, a head of lettuce for $.99, $2.49 worth of tomatoes, and a jar of pickles for $2.89. How much change did he get if he paid for these items with a $20 bill?

2. What will a man working 9 hours and 30 minutes earn if his rate of pay is $6.40 per hour?

3. One cup of a floor cleaner is to be mixed with 1 gallon of water. To clean a house, it will take four cups of cleaner. How much water will be needed to mix with that much cleaner?

4. A discount store sells everything at 25% off the list price. During an after-Christmas sale, the store took an additional 1/4 off. If the list price for a pair of shoes is $80.00, what would the shoes cost during the special sale?

5. On a map, a distance of 5 feet is represented by one inch. How long must a line be to represent a distance of 75 feet?

6. The speed limit on most interstate highways is 65 miles per hour. How far will a car travel in 7 hours at the legal speed limit?

7. Jerry purchased a boat for $2,500. He made a down payment of $500 and agreed to pay a 1 1/2% finance charge per month on the unpaid balance. How much did he owe at the end of the first month?

8. What is the diameter of the largest circle that can be drawn inside of a square with sides of 10 inches?

9. A soccer field is 130 yards by 100 yards. How much shorter is it to cross the soccer field diagonally than to walk around the two sides?

10. Let A stand for Amber's age. Her mother is 2 more than four times Amber's age. Write this as an algebraic expression.

11. $(10x^2-5x+3) - (7x^2-3x+5)$

ANSWERS AND EXPLANATIONS

1. Answer: $5.85
   First, add the four items and get a total of $14.14 and subtract the total from $20 to get $5.85.

2. Answer: $60.80
   Multiply $6.40 times 9.5 to get $60.80.

3. Answer: 4 gallons
   Use a proportion here of
   $$\frac{1 \text{ cup of cleaner}}{1 \text{ gallon water}} = \frac{4 \text{ cups cleaner}}{x \text{ gallons water}}$$
   Cross multiply and get $x = 4$

4. Answer: $45.00
   25% of 80 is 20. Subtract 20 from 80 (= 60) then take an additional 1/4 off the 60 (= 15). Subtract 15 from 60 = $45.00.

5. Answer: 15 inches
   Set this up in a proportion as follows:
   $\frac{1 \text{ inch}}{5 \text{ feet}} = \frac{x \text{ inches}}{75 \text{ feet}}$ (cross multiply to obtain $5x = 75$)
   then $x = 15$

6. Multiply 65 times 7 to obtain 455 miles.

7. Answer: $2,030.00
   Subtract $500 from $2,500 to get $2,000. Multiply .015 times $2,000 to get $30, then add $30 to $2,000 to obtain $2,030 as a balance at the end of the first month.

8. Answer: 10 inches.

10 inches

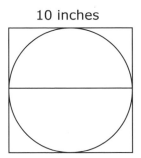

9. Answer: Approximately 66 yards
    Use the Pythagorean theorem to solve this problem.
    Square 100 and add it to 130 squared, then take the
    square root of it and subtract it from 230 to obtain
    approximately 66 yards.

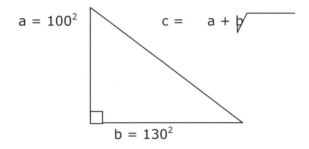

$a = 100^2$ $c = \quad a + b\sqrt{}$

$b = 130^2$

10. Answer: $4A + 2$
    Two more than a number means to add two, and
    four times can be written $4A$. Therefore, the expression
    is $4A + 2$.

11. Answer: $3x^2 - 2x - 2$. (Collect like terms.)

___

Whether you enjoyed the challenge of Judy's math review
or broke out in a cold sweat at the sight of it, you *can* do
college math. Again, colleges and universities have free
tutoring in the skills development centers. You can get help
there or buy a basic math computer program to brush up your
math skills. If you have children in school, helping them with
their math homework will give you lots of practice. They
might also help you.

Chapter 11

Taking Tests

You will probably have your first experience with testing before you enroll in your first class. Most schools now require placement assessments. Students who are over 25 years of age usually are not required to submit SAT or ACT scores; however, even with older students (who have a better success rate than younger students), testing is important in making sure students are prepared for the courses they take. Chapters 6, 7, and 8 will help you decide whether you want to brush up on your own before you take the college placement tests. (Don't wait too long, though. You may find that you will feel better prepared for college work if you go ahead and take the developmental courses in Math and/or English.) But, here we will talk about the tests you will take during your coursework.

Preparing for tests

Some students make good grades in high school because they have good memories for facts and formulas. College work, however, requires making inferences and synthesizing material. Chapter 6 offers help with preparing for tests, but here I will deal with mental preparation, and I will stress three important steps in preparing for tests. When you review for a test, make sure you understand the "big picture." For instance, suppose you are studying for a history test on the period of the

Spanish-American War. You know all the facts surrounding the incident, the parties involved—the Who, What, Where, When, and How. You have gathered all the evidence. Now it is time to evaluate the evidence, make connections, and draw conclusions about the events of the period. What were the immediate effects of the war? What were the long-term effects? How did war affect the foreign policy in America at the time? Was the effect a lasting effect? What can you say about the opposition to the war in 1899? Who opposed it and why? How did their predictions pan out? Were they right or wrong?

The point is that just knowing facts will not prepare you for, perhaps, a single essay question in which you must evaluate the effect of the Spanish-American War on American foreign policy. So, as you review, summarize your knowledge in social, political, and economical terms. The answers may be obvious after you have asked the right questions of yourself, but take time to ask the questions. You will be enriched for the effort, even if you end up with a multiple choice test that asks for facts.

Preparing Yourself Mentally

Mental preparation for a test begins long before the start of the test. If you allow your fears to get the best of you every time you think of the test situation, you will be psyching yourself up for a tough time. Although some anxiety is normal and helpful in keeping the mind alert to details, too much anxiety interferes with thinking processes. If you practice deep-breathing or other relaxation techniques such as tensing then relaxing muscles, you can use your time in a relaxed position to imagine yourself calmly succeeding on test day. Use time before the test to think positive thoughts about the test and ease anxiety. You might imagine taking the test in a peaceful place and in a comfortable position. Imagine the test as a pleasant experience in which you have a chance to respond to a challenge and show what you have learned.

You might also remember to wear comfortable clothing on test day. A belt that is cutting you in half or shoes that are pinching your little toe can be a distraction. Loosen a belt, unbutton the top button on your pants, take off the shoes—whatever it takes to be comfortable. Make sure you have the materials you will need—pen, pencil, paper, etc.—and that you arrive on time, and *listen carefully* to any instructions the teacher gives.

Note: Wear a watch so that you can pace yourself by allowing so much time for each section. Ignore anyone who finishes early; that person may have only answered half the questions. In fact, don't worry if you are the last one in the room, and don't let some instructor who is in a hurry to go eat lunch intimidate you into rushing.

If you have severe anxiety before a test, see the school counselor, who will have information on test anxiety. Mild anxiety might result from feeling—or being—ill prepared. If you have studied the material, relax and feel secure in the knowledge that you have learned something.

Objective Tests

There are many folk tales about objective tests. You might hear statements such as "Don't choose answers with the words *always, never, none, must* and *only*"; "Choose the answer that is longer than the other answers"; "Never choose the same letter on a multiple choice more than two times in a row"; "Never change an answer once you have written it"; etc. These adages are based mainly on superstition. Although words like *sometimes, often,* and *seldom* indicate that some exceptions are allowed, we can't always be sure they indicate a right answer. And though it is true that sometimes the first response to a question is correct, at other times careful analysis will reveal that the first response was wrong. It is important to read a question carefully, analyze it, and then choose a response based on knowledge rather than superstition.

Caution: When answering objective tests on a separate answer sheet, omitting the answer to a question can cause the remaining answers to be out of order and be counted as wrong. This is especially true of computer-graded tests. Computer answer sheets are used for most standardized tests, and the computer sees only a mark by a certain number. Pay special attention to the next answer you mark after skipping a question to make sure you have also left a blank for the answer. Skipping a particularly tough question with the thought of coming back to it later is okay, but find some way to identify those questions. On a computer scoring sheet, you might make tiny marks by the numbers of skipped questions and erase them after you have answered the question. Use any remaining time to check back over each answer and make sure the answer is actually for the question number it is next to.

Multiple-choice questions

When answering a multiple-choice question, read the statement carefully, making sure you understand the statement and looking for qualifiers such as *always* or *not* which limit answers. It is helpful to answer the question mentally before looking at the answer options. Read all the answers, eliminating the ones that are obviously wrong. Of the remaining answers, choose the most correct answer. You may find that more than one answer is correct, but one is more correct, or the correct answer is "All of the above" or "Both B and C." For that reason it is important to keep reading even after you have spotted an answer that you believe is correct.

When you are not sure of the correct answer, you can make informed guesses by eliminating as many answers as you can. Some tests have penalties for incorrect answers. For a test that has a high penalty for incorrect answers, you might use this strategy: if you can eliminate two answers that you believe are wrong, your chances of guessing the correct answer are raised to fifty percent, and you should go ahead and guess.

True/false questions

When responding to a true/false statement, read the statement carefully to make sure it is *all* true or *all* false. Part of a statement might be true, for instance, while another part of it might be false, making the entire statement false.

A true/false statement can be incorrect in the following ways:

1. It may identify one term or date with the wrong definition or fact.
2. It may contain something that is wrong.
3. It may join two terms that are not related as stated.

Ignore any superstitions about the arrangement of true/false answers. Don't think you must be wrong if you have marked most of the answers true or most of them false of if there is a distinct pattern of alternating true answers and false answers. Read each question carefully and trust you own knowledge in answering. If you do not know the answer, you have a 50 percent chance of guessing the right answer. But you can increase your chances by making informed guesses, by analyzing the question carefully. You may also find clues in other questions in the test. If you put question marks in the margins next to questions you are not sure of, you can come back to them when you have finished the other questions.

Matching questions

Use the process of elimination for matching tests by crossing out each answer as you use it. For some tests, you will not be permitted to mark on the test booklet, but if you are allowed to have scrap paper, you can jot down the answers as you use them. If you are not absolutely sure of an answer you use, put a question mark by it. You may need to re-evaluate several of your choices if you find that you must change one answer. For tests on which the answers may be used more than once, you can compare the two questions for which you have used an answer to make sure they are related.

Short-answer questions

Since short-answer, or fill-in-the-blank, tests usually require memorization of facts, you might refer to the section in Chapter 6 on memorization techniques. Flash cards are especially helpful to visual learners, and they can be used to study terms and definitions or other kinds of matched information.

You might also try "chunking" and "clustering" pieces of information. When chunking, cut off manageable pieces of information to study separately. To cluster, link four or five related facts to study together.

Any fact or bit of information you can relate to your own experience will be more easily remembered. For instance, if you are trying to remember the date that the telephone was invented (1876) and who invented it (Alexander Graham Bell), you might look at the trademark on your telephone at home, notice that it includes the name Bell, visualize Ma Bell as Alexander's wife, and think about the telephone as being 125 (2001-1876=125), or so, years old. (One very good student advises to never leave a blank space on a fill-in-the-blank test, even if you have to write your mother's maiden name in the blank.)

Note: When your test is returned, always check to make sure each answer that was marked incorrect is actually wrong. People make mistakes. If you are given back only your answers, ask the instructor to let you see a copy of the test key to check your answers.

Essay tests

Essay tests are favored by college teachers because these tests reveal many things about a student's ability. They reveal a student's

1. ability to learn and recall information,
2. ability to interpret and analyze information,
3. understanding of the subject,
4. reasoning behind the answers,
5. ability to organize ideas,
6. creativity, and
7. ability to use the conventions of written English.

Before you tackle an essay question, make sure you have studied it carefully. Some questions must be taken apart and analyzed to be understood thoroughly. Look for key words such as those listed below:

Key Word	Task
Argue	Choose a side of an issue and give reasons to support your stance
Analyze	Break something apart and discuss the parts
Compare	Point out similarities between two things, people, ideas, etc.

Contrast	Point out differences between two things, people, ideas, etc.
Define or Describe	Classify the subject and give specific details about something or someone
Illustrate	Explain fully, providing examples, reasons, etc. (show, prove, demonstrate, discuss, etc.)
Evaluate	Judge the topic for its truth, significance, etc. and justify your assessment
Summarize	Give an overview of the main points related to a topic
Trace	In chronological order, describe the development or progress related to a specific topic

Essay test answers have what all good writing has: an introduction, a body, and a conclusion. A statement of the main idea in the introduction tells the reader what the essay is about. Paragraphs contain ideas and details that are closely related. Transitions help the reader shift from one idea to another. A summary conclusion reminds the reader of the main idea of the essay.

Making a brief outline on scrap paper will help guide your writing. Since you will probably not have time to recopy the essay, it is important that you do your organization work before you begin. The key verb in the question will sometimes dictate the organization. For instance, if you are asked to compare or contrast, the organization might be whole-to-whole—talk about the aspects of one subject then talk about the other subject—or part-to-part—talk about one aspect of both subjects, then deal with another aspect, and so on. If you are asked to trace the development of something or another, the order will be chronological. Making a list of the incidents or developments you want to include in your essay will make your writing task easier. Simply go down the list, including one item after another in your response.

The writing process must be abbreviated during essay exams. You don't have the luxury of extensive revision. But you can still allow a portion of your time for each stage of the writing process, perhaps allowing the first fifteen minutes of an hour-long period to brainstorm ideas and organize them into a logical sequence. You could then draft your essay, using the informal outline you have made and periodically reading back over what you have written. You can use the last five or ten minutes of the exam time to proofread and correct your essay(s).

Test anxiety

Since you are an adult and you take seriously the education you are paying for, you will probably be more than a little up-tight about the first tests you take in college. Actually, there are several reasons that you may have test anxiety. I'll list them here:

1. You take the test seriously (perhaps too seriously) because
    a. You may feel a personal attachment—in other words, you may feel (even subconsciously) that how well you do on a test reflects your worth as a person;
    b. You are paying for the course and don't want to fail and waste your money;
    c. You are a mature person and tend to take the whole college experience seriously; and
    d. You are responsible enough to take full credit or blame for what you do.

2.   You are not used to taking a test; it is a new and somewhat strange position to be in.

3.   You may not feel that you know how to study for a test.

4.   You may not feel that you have time to study for a test.

Although test anxiety will diminish somewhat as you take more and more tests, test anxiety is something that you can control from the beginning. The following material is designed to prepare you for the different kinds of test situations.

Testing is not designed to torture you. If you really think about it, you have taken and survived many tests since the time you first began to function as a person. Babies test themselves first by trying a few paces and then by moving a longer distance. They show pleasure at meeting each new challenge, at learning each new skill and proving they can master it. Humans are tested and test themselves in many ways. Ultimately, they are demonstrating certain skills. In the college test situation, you will be showing that

1.   you can control your mental and physical functions in a test situation,
2.   you can follow written or verbal instructions, and
3.   you can use higher-order thinking skills in analyzing both the question and your response.

All this is in addition to showing that you know the answers to the questions—that you have learned something.

But in order to do any of these things, you must first exert control over yourself, over your mental functions and the corresponding physical functions. For example, a person who is not in control may give way to worst-case fears, may let her mind wander through all the possible nightmare situations—everything from falling flat on her face as she enters the test room to having a total mental blackout when handed the test. Mental fears can result in physical handicaps: the heart may beat wildly, resulting in a preoccupation with the fear of having a stroke or cardiac arrest; profuse sweating may cause a preoccupation with wondering whether or not the Ban is working; trembling hands may result in almost illegible handwriting and cause a preoccupation with actually forming letters, something that should be done with little mental energy.

In other words, every thought that is not related to the test itself consumes valuable mental energy. The idea is to put the fears aside so that you can use everything you have to meet the challenge, to demonstrate what you have learned. So, first, we will talk about emotional preparation for the test situation.

Emotional Preparation

1. When you think about an upcoming test, shove any negative emotions out of your mind and replace them with positive ones. Try visualizing yourself taking the test in a peaceful setting. Think of sitting on a beach under a palm tree or on a porch swing in a country cabin— wherever you think you can feel relaxed. Take deep breaths and consciously control your physical responses. Feel your heart slow down and your muscles relax. Later, when you actually are in the testing room, recall this relaxed feeling.

2. Put the exam in proper perspective. It is only a test, one of the hundreds you have already taken in your life. How well you do does not reflect your intelligence or worth as a person. You have done many things in your life. You've shown courage in facing labor pains and death, war and pestilence, taxes and overdue bills. A test is just a test. You have a chance to prove how well you have prepared

yourself. But whether or not you pass the course usually does not hinge on one test.

3.   Practice taking tests. Take the quizzes in magazines—Family Circle, Cosmopolitan, etc.—for fun. Enjoy the act of analyzing the question itself and then responding from what you know about yourself. Practice making up your own test questions and answers over the material you are studying (discussed in the next section).

4.   Learn to study like the pros. (See Chapter 6 and the suggestions below.)

5.   Learn to manage your time so that you can feel comfortable during the time you are studying without worrying about the other things you should be doing.

6.   Think of the test as an exciting challenge—a chance to prove to yourself that you know the material. Although your instructor may be a giant in his or her field and a nice person that you want to impress, the person who is most important in this situation is yourself. You want to do well on the test for *your* personal satisfaction and for *your* personal goals. And a particular test will not be your last chance to achieve your goals.

Taking Tests   239

Mental Preparation

The biggest cause of test anxiety (and other kinds of anxiety) is not feeling in control. You can exert control over your emotions and body by practicing the suggestions above. To exert control over your thinking, you must know the material. The study techniques in Chapter 6 will help you in preparing mentally for tests, but here are some additional suggestions:

1. Ask the instructor beforehand whether the test will be objective or essay. As you study the material for a test, try to predict what the instructor might ask on a test. You might even make up your own set of test questions.
2. Write out answers to any study questions you are given. You will be reinforcing the ideas and information you need to know and practicing the kind of thinking you will be doing in the test situation.
3. After you have studied the material, relax and feel confident in your knowledge. You can schedule a time for review to reinforce what you have learned, but you have done your best for this stage of preparation. Remember that you are in control. You have decided how much time you can devote to preparing for the exam. Yes, there will be some instructors who delight in making tests that students will fail. Just remember: Everything that goes around comes around. You can't control the instructor. But you are controlling yourself. Yes, there may be a question that you cannot answer no matter how much time you devote to your study. But you have taken reasonable steps to prepare yourself for the exam, which is only one of the things in your busy life.

Going into the test situation

1.   Make sure that you have had a good night's sleep. Don't schedule the evening before an exam to study. Do your studying at least two days before the exam. On the day before the exam, schedule review time during the day or early in the evening, and then relax. Feel confident in your knowledge. Of course you don't know everything there is to know about the subject, but no one does.

2.   Go to class early, allowing enough time for traffic and unforeseen delays. Being rushed for time and worrying that you will be late builds anxiety. Once at school, you can find a quiet place to go over your key words and brief summary. Try to block out any confusing chatter or speculations about what might be on the exam. You are prepared; trust yourself.

3.   Take adequate supplies for the test. Make sure you have plenty of notebook paper and extra pens and pencils. Many instructors use scantron sheets for objective tests, and you will need #2 pencils for them. Take pens that have dark blue or black ink and write smoothly. For math tests, you might need other kinds of supplies such as calculators, rulers, etc. Make sure you have your textbook, also. Instructors have been known to say, at the last minute, that it's okay to use your text. Using the text won't rescue those who are not prepared. Flipping through pages takes time. But you may feel better to know that you have the book and that you can refer to it if you want to use a specific quotation, for instance.
    You will also want to have a watch so that you can control the amount of time you devote to each question and know exactly how much time you have left. The idea

is not to constantly check the watch and be preoccupied with the passing of each minute but to *control* the amount of time you have for the test and make sure you don't lose points because you get carried away with answering a particular question.

4. Use a sheet of paper for scrap paper to write down notes. If you are given an exam and expected to write on that sheet and have no other paper out, use the back side of the sheet for notes.

5. Listen carefully to verbal instructions given by the instructor. If you are not sure you understand an instruction, ask for clarification, and don't worry about how the question sounds to others. The instructor may tell which questions to answer or say something about the order in which the questions should be answered.

6. Read the test instructions carefully before starting. Know exactly what is expected. Put your name on your paper. It is easy to forget later when you are so relieved at having finished the test.

Tips for taking essay exams

Whereas objective (multiple choice, etc.) exams assess how well a student recalls information, essay exams allow the instructor to assess many things. In addition to recalling information for an essay exam, the student must be able to analyze and interpret the information she has studied. She also must be able to apply the information in writing a logically organized response. The instructor can see in the answer the reasoning behind the answer. Not only does the student give an answer (that on an objective test could be a mere guess) but the student also explains the answer and shows real understanding. In order to write a coherent response to an essay question, a student must be able to use basic writing skills (Ch. 7) and the conventions of usage and punctuation (Ch. 8). Mastering basic writing skills is something you can work on well before you begin to take a test. During the test, your mental energies should be focused on presenting a well-organized and creative response to the exam questions.

1. Read all questions through before starting to answer. As you read each question, look for key words such as *define, compare, discuss*, etc., and underline these words. Jot down on scrap paper or next to the question any words or ideas that come to mind that you might use later in your answer. If you are allowed to choose certain questions, put a star by the questions that you feel most comfortable answering. As you read the questions, look for relationships between the questions, and decide what the instructor's overall aim seems to be. Does he seem to be more interested in details than in summary-type responses? Does she want you to apply certain basic principles (such as a certain kind of literary analysis or a certain school of thought) in your responses? When you read all the questions, the answers will be "cooking" in your subconscious mind as you respond to specific questions. If you are given a choice of questions, you can quickly blank out a question that you will not respond to and use your subconscious cooking for only those that you have put a star next to.

    If the questions are assigned points, decide how much time you can devote to each question, based on the number of points. For instance, if you can choose four 25 point questions from the list and you have one hour in which to take the test, you know that you should not devote more than 15 minutes to each question.

2. When you are ready to start responding to the questions, begin by answering the easiest one first if you are not told to answer the questions in a certain order. This will allow for more cooking time for the more difficult questions. Read the question word-by-word, perhaps moving your lips as you read. This is to make sure you don't overlook a little word like *not* that changes the whole question.

3. Write the number of the question, and reword the question to use in your answer. For instance, if the question says, "Discuss the effects of World War II on the American family," you might begin your response with, "World War II affected the structure of the American family." But before you begin to respond to the question, make a little list of details you would want to include. This list can be in the form of an outline, but you won't have time to worry about numbers and letters. Indenting words can show relationships:

> Before war
> Role of
>> men
>> women
>> children
> During war
> Men absent
> Women working
> Children—more responsibility

Your statement about family life before the war is mainly to show contrast; the question relates to what happened during the war and how it affected family life after the war. You want to focus your attention on how the absence of men and the changing roles of women and children changed the family structure. You might want to jot down details under the subtopics in your outline. Remember to refer to your outline as you begin each new paragraph and keep your answer tightly focused; do not get off on a tangent about today's women's liberation movement, for instance. What you will be doing in your answer is writing a thesis statement (a statement of the main idea of your response) and explaining it. Give examples, reasons, and any hard facts you can tie in to support your argument that World War II affected the American family. After you have built a case, summarize it with a conclusion that is directly related to your beginning thesis statement.

4. As you respond to the questions and make your lists of possible ideas, check each one against the questions. If some ideas don't relate directly, mark through them with a line. Make sure you answer the question as it is asked, not as you would like for it to be asked. Just because you happen to know more about the effect of World War II on American women doesn't mean your response should focus on women. The question was about the family, and women are a part of that whole.

5. If you aren't sure at first about a long, complex question, break it down in parts, analyzing each part before relating it to the whole. Sometimes you may think at first you don't know the answer, but with a little brainstorming of possible ideas, you will come up with the solution to the problem. Sometimes a question might seem very difficult when, in fact, it is simple and the answer is obvious.

6. If you are doing answers in order and you run across one that you can't answer easily, leave space for the answer and move on to the next question. Spending time wrestling with it will be frustrating and take time away from writing the answers you do know. You may get ideas for the answer after you have finished the other questions, when you are more relaxed and confident that you have written other good answers.

7. If you forget to budget your time for each question and run out of time, write an answer in outline form for a question that you can't answer with a full essay. At least the instructor will know that you know the information and might give at least partial credit for your outline.

8. Use any time you have left to read over your answers. Make sure you actually wrote what you thought you wrote—that you didn't leave out words or phrases. Check to make sure your sentences are complete and that they are correctly punctuated.

Math Exams

The guidelines for taking math tests are much the same as for taking essay tests. Instead of responding with an essay, you will be responding with a solution. The process of finding the correct answer is important and usually will be written on your exam instead of on scrap paper.

Tips for taking objective exams

Objective tests are mainly to measure your knowledge of factual information. They do not measure how well you can organize a written response or how creative you can be. Yet objective tests can require careful analysis and interpretation.

Some questions might be referred to as "trick" questions because they require a little more thought and careful reading. Multiple choice, matching, true-false, and fill-in-the-blank are all kinds of objective tests. Often you will have a combination of kinds of questions, including essay questions.

1.   When responding to objective test questions, you will need to go in order. It is not necessary to try to read all the questions before starting to answer although you should keep in mind that one question might include information that will help answer another one. However, if there are no time limitations, it is always good to read through all the questions to get a general overview of the test.

2.   As you work through the questions, make sure you read each word. Pay special attention to words like *not*. You might be asked to choose the answer that is correct or to choose the answer that is not correct. Also pay special attention to words such as *always, all, none*, and *never*. These words *may* be a signal that the answer is incorrect, but not always.

3.   When you read a question, think of the correct answer before you read the options on a multiple choice or matching test. But even when you find the answer that matches yours, check the others to make sure that another answer is not more complete.

4.   If you aren't sure of an answer, eliminate answers that you know are not correct, then choose between the remaining answers. If you don't have any idea which answer is correct, guess—unless there is a very high penalty for guessing. One successful teacher advises to always

choose the same letter on guesses so you will have a built in percentage of correct guesses.

5. Trust your instincts. If you have selected an answer after a careful reading of all the answers, move on. Later, you may have time to come back to it and reread it, but unless you discover something that you missed in the first place, don't change it.

6. Use any time you have left to check your answers. Make sure you have numbered correctly and haven't skipped an answer. Be especially careful with scantron answer sheets that you have left a blank for each question you didn't answer.

Works Cited

Gibaldi, Joseph. *MLA Handbook for Writers of Research Papers*. 4th ed.. New York: The Modern Language Association of America, 1995.

Apps, Jerold W. *Study Skills for Adults Returning to School*. New York: McGraw, 1982.

Buzan, Tony. *Use Both Sides of Your Brain*. New York: Dutton, 1983.

Duffy, James P. *Cutting College Costs*. New York: Barnes and Noble, 1988.

Feder, Bernard. *The Complete Guide to Taking Tests*. Englewood Cliffs: Prentice, 1979.

Gazzaniga, Michael. *The Social Brain: Discovering the Networks of the Mind*. New York: Basic, 1985.

Green, Gordon W., Jr. *Getting Straight A's*. New York: Carol, 1985.

Hannel, G. Ivan and Lee Hannel. "The Seven Steps to Critical Thinking: A Practical Application of Critical Thinking Skills." *Bulletin*, May, 1998.

Joyce, Bruce. "Models for Teaching Thinking." *Educational Leadership*. May, 1985.

Kahn, Norma B. *More Learning in Less Time*. 3rd ed. Berkeley: Ten Speed, 1989.

Schart-Hunt, Diana and Pam Hait. *Studying Smart*. New York: HarperCollins, 1990.

Sylvester, Robert. "Research on Memory: Major Discoveries, Major Educational Challenges." *Educational Leadership*. April, 1985.

Index